NOTRE DAME
AND THE
CIVIL WAR

NOTRE DAME
AND THE
CIVIL WAR

Marching Onward to Victory

JAMES M. SCHMIDT

Charleston   London

THE
History
PRESS

Published by The History Press
Charleston, SC 29403
www.historypress.net

Copyright © 2010 by James M. Schmidt
All rights reserved

First published 2010

Manufactured in the United States

ISBN 978.1.59629.879.8

Library of Congress Cataloging-in-Publication Data

Schmidt, James M., 1964-
Notre Dame and the Civil War : marching onward to victory / James M. Schmidt.
p. cm.
Includes bibliographical references.
ISBN 978-1-59629-879-8
1. University of Notre Dame--History--19th century. 2. Indiana--History--Civil War, 1861-1865. 3. United States--History--Civil War, 1861-1865--Education and the war. I. Title.
E541.N6S36 2010
977.2'03--dc22
2010041016

To my cousin, Father Peter Meis, OFM, Cap., in admiration of his more than forty years of devoted and loving missionary work to the indigenous peoples of Papua New Guinea.

CONTENTS

PREFACE

I did not attend the University of Notre Dame, but like millions of other Americans I happily count myself among its "subway alumni"—the legion of fans with a special affinity for the home of the "Fighting Irish" due to their personal religious traditions, the school's sports tradition or, as in my case, both. That affinity only grew stronger when I became more familiar with Notre Dame's long, remarkable and patriotic record of supporting our country in wartime. In writing this book about the interesting and important role that Notre Dame played in the Civil War, it is my fervent hope that its heroes of the battlefield will be as well known as its heroes of the playing field.

The book is the product of more than a decade's interest and research and the kind, enthusiastic and expert cooperation and support of many people, including, first and foremost, the wonderful staff of the University of Notre Dame Archives, especially Kevin Cawley, Peter Lysy, Sharon Sumpter and Elizabeth Hogan, who have answered questions and supplied me with a host of material for many years. Sister Bernice Hollenhorst (Archives and Records of the Sisters of the Congregation of the Holy Cross) and Deb Buzzard and Father James Connelly (Archives of the Indiana Province of the Congregation of the Holy Cross) also provided advice, documents and photographs from their wonderful collections.

The story of the University of Notre Dame is intimately connected to the story of the state of Indiana. As such, the assistance of the following people was essential and much appreciated: Suzanne Hahn of the Indiana

Historical Society; Diana Zornow of the Elkhart County (Indiana) Historical Museum; and Susan Lowery of the Mishawaka (Indiana) Heritage Center. The reference staff—especially Patricia Bicknell—at my hometown Montgomery County (Texas) Memorial Library were friendly and helpful as always.

Tim Deichl was a kind and early supporter of this project and provided rare documents and photographs related to his family history—especially important were items concerning Notre Dame student-soldier, and Union general, William F. Lynch. Likewise, Linda Fluharty shared her remarkable genealogical research on student-soldier Michael Quinlan. Jay Odom, proprietor of www.civilwardocs.com, expertly retrieved soldier service records from the National Archives. Dave Powell, author, historian and battlefield tour guide, kindly shared correspondence from his collection regarding the Battle of Chickamauga.

Professional photographer Pat Brownewell, Notre Dame graduate and navy veteran Corrine Rypka, author and historian Michael Aubrecht, historical marker expert Craig Swain and lifelong friend Curtis Fears all kindly provided much-needed (and excellent) modern photographs of monuments and memorials from Indiana, Pennsylvania, Missouri and Washington, D.C., of Notre Dame's service in the war.

In all of my writing endeavors, I have received the generous advice and support of professional and academic historians, and this project was no different. Dr. Dorothy Pratt of the University of South Carolina kindly provided her unpublished—and essential—manuscript regarding the effect of the draft on Notre Dame in the Civil War. Dr. John F. Marszalek, Professor Emeritus, Mississippi State University—and executive director of the Ulysses S. Grant Association—read the manuscript and provided expert comments and sage advice that made the final work all the better.

Guy R. Hasegawa—dear friend, estimable author and historian in his own right and expert editor—applied his sharp eye and blue pencil to the manuscript but mostly offered me his encouragement.

Joseph Gartrell, my editor at The History Press, saw merit in this project and championed its publication, and for that—and his friendship—I am most grateful.

My wife Susan; our children Katherine, Robert and Michael; and my parents, brothers, sisters, in-laws, grandparents, aunts, uncles and other family and friends provided loving support as always. The dedication to my cousin, Father Peter Meis, OFM, Cap., is both sincere and fitting: His work among the native people of Papua New Guinea is a modern example of the same missionary zeal that brought the founders of Notre Dame from France to our shores and its Holy Cross priests to the camps and battlefields of the Civil War; it is a privilege to call him family.

Any errors in editing, fact or interpretation are mine alone.

While this book may be the *product* of a decade's work, it is by no means the *culmination* of my research or interest in the interesting and important role of Notre Dame in the Civil War. It is and will be a lifelong passion, and there is still much to learn. Chief among my goals is to document as many of the Notre Dame student-soldiers as possible. I encourage readers to contact me through the publisher or through my "Notre Dame in the Civil War" website at http://notredamecivilwar.blogspot.com.

INTRODUCTION

The peaks of Notre Dame history are shrouded in the mists of war.
—Father Hugh O'Donnnell, president, University of Notre Dame, 1941

On March 4, 1861, nineteen-year-old college student Orville Chamberlain wrote a letter home with the opening line: "We are having 'recreation' here this afternoon in honor of 'Old Abe's' inauguration." Apart from mention of the nation's new president, there was no other hint of campus talk regarding news or politics. Indeed, the balance of his letter related to the timeless concerns of any college student: learning to live on his own, his classmates, his studies, the quality and quantity of the food and—of course—his need for money. When Confederate guns fired on Fort Sumter only weeks later, everything changed for Chamberlain and for his school, the University of Notre Dame.[1]

In fact, few institutions of higher education can boast of the sacrifices made by the University of Notre Dame, which—like Orville Chamberlain—was only nineteen years old when the war began. Over the course of four years, Notre Dame gave freely of its faculty and students as soldiers, sent its Holy Cross priests to the camps and battlefields as chaplains and dispatched its sisters to the hospitals as nurses; some of the boys, men and women made the ultimate sacrifice and never returned.

Though far from the battlefields itself, the war was still ever-present on campus, as Notre Dame witnessed fisticuffs among the student body, provided a home to the children of a famous general, responded to political harassment and tried to keep at least some of its community out of the fray. When the war was over, a proud Notre Dame welcomed back several bona fide war heroes—including Orville Chamberlain, who earned the Medal of Honor—and became home to a unique veteran's organization.

The school's participation in the Civil War established a tradition of "Fighting Irish" tenacity on the battlefield by its student-soldiers and spiritual strength imparted by its priests and sisters. That tradition was set from the start by the example and abilities of two people: Father Edward Sorin and Mother Angela Gillespie.

The Fighting French

Although the University of Notre Dame has established a thoroughly Irish character for more than a century, it actually traces its roots to France and the founding of the Congregation of the Holy Cross in the 1840s by Abbé Basil Moreau. Among the young men attracted to Moreau's order was Edward Sorin. Born in 1814 at Ahuillé, France, where his mother directed his early education in the classics, Sorin felt a calling to the priesthood, entered the seminary and distinguished himself in his ability and example. Upon his ordination, he was inspired by reports of missionaries in foreign lands, especially in the Far East but also in the United States. Though Father Sorin was only in his twenties and but recently ordained, Father Moreau selected him to establish a foothold in America for the order.

Father Sorin and a small band of brothers of the order set sail from France on August 8, 1841, and arrived in New York in mid-September. After a rest of a few days, they set out for Vincennes, in southwest Indiana. The bishop there—responsible for the entire state—had asked Abbé Moreau to send Holy Cross priests and brothers to minister to Indiana's growing Catholic population. A year later, Father Sorin received permission to establish a college at the site of an abandoned missionary outpost in the wilderness of northwestern Indiana. On November 26, 1842, Father Sorin and his cadre arrived at a small clearing neighboring a body of water named Ste. Marie des Laces by the French missionaries who had once ministered to the Native American Potawatomi in the area. Father Sorin christened the site Notre Dame du Lac (Our Lady of the Lake), a name that would also be attached to the university.

Father Edward Sorin, CSC, founder of the University of Notre Dame. *Priests of Holy Cross, Indiana Province Archives Center.*

Nearly two years passed before Father Sorin could erect buildings and organize a faculty. In 1844, the state granted the university a charter. Although the school was now empowered to grant degrees in the liberal arts and sciences and in law and medicine, the first instruction was given only in the studies thought best to furnish a general education: philosophy, history, mathematics and languages. In fact, as the nearby educational conditions were as primitive as the environs themselves, Father Sorin established a preparatory school so that the young men could then take up college work. He also established a faculty in theology to prepare men for the priesthood and a "Manual Labor" school for the destitute and orphans. Neal Gillespie—later Father Neal—received the university's first bachelor's degree in 1849.

Campus of the University of Notre Dame, circa 1860. *University of Notre Dame Archives.*

Notre Dame was plagued by early misfortune, including fires, debt, disease and disagreements with the Holy Cross mother house in France. Yet by prayer, the intercession of its patrons—heavenly and temporal—the support of the citizens of nearby South Bend and, mostly, the confidence and competence of its founder, Father Sorin, the school began to grow. At first, the number of students at Notre Dame was small—fewer than seventy in 1850—with most coming from only a few states in the Midwest. By 1861, on the eve of the Civil War, the number had advanced to more than two hundred.

SISTER SCHOOL

In 1841, Abbé Moreau founded a group of religious women—the Sisters of the Holy Cross—to further the aims of his mission, and in 1843, he sent four of the sisters to Indiana to assist the Holy Cross priests at the fledgling University of Notre Dame. The sisters started to teach the local girls in Bertrand, Michigan, a river town just north of South Bend, Indiana, where they established St. Mary's Academy. In 1855, they moved the school to Indiana, near Notre Dame. By 1860, there were nearly two hundred sisters in the Holy Cross congregation serving the university, St. Mary's Academy, and a growing immigrant population.

Sister Mary of St. Angela (née Eliza Maria Gillespie), Mother Superior of the Sisters of the Holy Cross and St. Mary's Academy. *Sisters of the Holy Cross Records and Archives.*

Just as Father Sorin proved to be a steady and inspiring influence to the students and Holy Cross priests and brothers at Notre Dame, so too did the Holy Cross sisters and St. Mary's have an equally influential figure in Mother Angela Gillespie. Born in 1824 in Pennsylvania, Eliza Marie Gillespie was the daughter of a wealthy and prominent family. Her kin included brother Neal (Notre Dame's first graduate) and the politically connected Ewing family of Ohio.

Eliza finished her early schooling in Washington, D.C. Beautiful, vivacious and energetic, she might have become politically connected and powerful herself through marriage, but instead she pursued a religious vocation and joined the Sisters of the Holy Cross in 1853, taking the name Sister Angela. In addition to her piety and charity, Sister Angela also had considerable business and executive talents, having managed her stepfather's farm. Father Sorin thought her the ideal candidate to be superior of St. Mary's Academy, a position that she assumed in 1855.

The story of Notre Dame in the Civil War is an epic one: more than one hundred individual professors, students, priests or sisters served as soldiers, chaplains or nurses on battlefields, in camps or in hospitals in the thousand miles between Mississippi and Pennsylvania. This book aims to tell that story in the voices of the men and women who lived it.

Chapter 1

WARS AND RUMORS
OF WARS

Contrary to all the anticipations of thinking men, war broke out at the beginning of spring…and before the end of the year more than a million men had taken up arms, each in defense of his rights.

—Father Edward Sorin, 1861

F or more than fifteen years the South had been complaining of the North, and every year the Union seemed to be threatened. Men in Congress were accustomed to those threats, which had come to be but little regarded," wrote Father Sorin in 1861 of the great national questions of states' rights and slavery. While Notre Dame was far removed from the august halls of Congress, the campus was literally at a crossroads of the debate: two major routes of the Underground Railroad came through South Bend, and the Bulla farmhouse on campus was a "station" on the escape route of enslaved African Americans. Whether or not war was inevitable, the young men at Notre Dame were prepared for one.[2]

A FINE BODY OF MEN

Military units had existed on many college campuses for years before the Civil War, but the activity increased in the late 1850s. Some critics dismissed the activities as little more than a ploy to attract the admiring glances of young ladies, while others concluded that it was a "presentiment of war that aroused a new enthusiasm" for drilling.

Whatever the reason, the tradition at Notre Dame can be traced to the 1850s, when the first student-organized company could be seen marching across campus. For his part, Father Sorin encouraged the exercises not out of a pugnacious nature but rather for the "excellent physical training and gentlemanly bearing and manner which they were calculated to impart to the young men."[3]

In 1858, the *Chicago Daily Times* reported that "[Notre Dame] students have just finished organizing…a military company, which already numbers some forty or fifty members, and, I think, that even in Chicago, a city which has always been noted for its military tastes and science, they would be called a remarkably fine looking body of young men." If the company already struck a smart appearance, it was to get sharper still with the arrival that same year of William F. Lynch, a student from Elgin, Illinois.[4]

Lynch had been active in his hometown military company, which had one of the best drillmasters in the country. He became so enamored of the amateur soldier's life that he neglected his studies. Indeed, his father sent him to Notre Dame in no small part to "get him away from the glamour of the Elgin uniform." Lynch left the Elgin unit only to join another at Notre Dame and soon became the leader. Inspired by his experience at home, he changed the name of the company to the Notre Dame Continental Cadets and adopted a dress that was "very picturesque, beautiful and showy" in the style of the members' Revolutionary forefathers, as one student wrote:

> *The coat was of blue, with buff facing and braiding, and buttons of brass; the vest was buff and the necktie was white. The breeches were of blue cloth and came down to the knee, where they were fastened with brass buttons. The stockings of white reached to the knee, while the tops of the boots were ornamented with buff. The hat was three-cornered, ornamented with a red and white cockade.*[5]

"Not to be outdone by their seniors, the younger students clamored for the privilege of learning how to carry a gun," a Notre Dame historian wrote, and they formed their own company, which they styled the Washington Cadets. The school financial ledger for 1859–60 shows several expenses on behalf of the companies, including $36.00 for coats to Chicago tailor F.H. Taylor, $3.37 for tassels, $2.00 for gold lace and $32.50 for "work made by the Sisters of St. Mary's."[6]

For his part, student Neal Gillespie saw the younger boys' participation in the military company as a mixed blessing. When family friend "Franky" Bigelow was elected captain, Gillespie wrote to his mother: "[W]hether it will be a benefit for him I cannot say...holding a <u>high</u> position in it, his mind...will be taken up a great deal with it; and his regular classes will suffer for awhile at least." Still, he admitted, "the habit of strict regularity required by military law [and] the sometimes fatiguing drills will compensate in his physical education what he may lose for the present in his studies."[7]

The Continental Cadets finished the 1859 school year with an impressive display in the streets of Mishawaka, Indiana, which was enthusiastically reported in the pages of the *St. Joseph County Forum*:

> *The sound of martial music proceeding from the railroad depot, falling on the ears of the inhabitants of the neat little town...aroused them somewhat from their torpor...The music approached, and anon was heard above the music's sound the loud voice of a military commandant. Nearer and nearer the sounds approached and now was seen floating in the morning breeze the "Stars and Stripes" of the American union. And now appeared in full view the "Notre Dame Continental Cadets," commanded by Capt. R. Healy, assisted by Lts. Runnion, Miller, and Lynch.*
>
> *The company preceded by their martial band...marched in the most superior order through the principal streets performing various military evolutions, in such a masterly manner as would have done credit to any company in our large eastern cities.*

The cadets had some time before a formal dinner that evening and used the hours to "see what was to be seen in town" in small groups. The newspaper reported with admiration that "the Notre Dame cadets...quietly and cheerfully moved through the streets. They visited no saloons." At dinner, the cadet officers offered their congratulations on the success of the day's events and their compliments to their hosts, one of whom—Father Patrick Dillon, vice-president of Notre Dame—commented on the prevailing attitude of anti-Catholicism in the country and the school's demonstration against that prejudice in the morning's parade:

> *Today I feel proud that an Institution conducted by those who are too frequently branded as hostile to American Institutions and American*

liberty, has sent out a brilliant array of American youths clad in the costume of their revered ancestors—led on by that flag, than which on the wide face of the earth none is more honored. I say I feel proud. And gentleman, justly may I say so…your appearance before your fellow citizens today is to my mind a solid testimony of the fact, that while you are taught at Notre Dame to place all your hopes of success in an all wise Providence…you are there too taught to revere the memory of your sires, to cherish the precious boon they have purchased for you at the expense of their lives—that you are taught to defend with the last drop of your hearts blood that Liberty so dearly bought.[8]

Less than two years later, many of those very cadets—only then "playing at soldier"—would indeed defend that liberty.

WAR!

"Here all are well except those who are taken violently with the war fever, which epidemic rages in these northern climes in spite of the gloomy weather as fiercely as in the sunny south," wrote Father Neal Gillespie to his mother from Notre Dame on April 19, 1861, just days after the surrender of Fort Sumter and President Abraham Lincoln's first call for troops. "Some of the students perhaps will go to fight the battles of their country," he added but guessed that "the number will…be very small." He reported, with chagrin, that "the excitement has sadly interfered with the lessons of some of the hotheaded ones" but wrote with admiration of two young boys—family friends—who "[took] the matter coolly, as sensible young men" and did not "exhibit a very bellicose spirit nor vapor much about 'blood and thunder' and the 'cannon roar' and such like."[9]

One student with a decided "bellicose spirit" was William F. Lynch, commander of Notre Dame's Continental Cadets. The citizens of nearby South Bend met at the St. Joseph County Courthouse on the evening of April 15, 1861, to determine their course of action. With party loyalties set aside, the citizenry stood shoulder to shoulder in the packed courtroom, but Lynch—who was in the hall—grew impatient with the speeches and platitudes. He then gave a speech "full of a fiery patriotism that carried the audience with his enthusiasm," one historian declared. Years later, the *Notre Dame Scholastic* recalled the thrilling scene:

He stood up, tall, soldierly; his Irish eyes were glittering, his face pale. The vibrant ring of the first sentence he rattled out above the heads of the good citizens made them catch their breath. In five minutes they were frantic; and when the boy told them he was going to the front to shed the last drop of his blood if needed for the Union, the audience leaped to its feet; cheer after cheer rang out wildly. [10]

Lynch then returned to Notre Dame, where as one report stated, he "set his own cadets afire, or rather…let the blaze out—they were afire already. To a boy they wanted to go to the front by the next train and put down the uprising of the South at once." Lynch left for Indianapolis to offer Notre Dame's military company to the state, but Governor Oliver P. Morton was already overwhelmed with like petitions, and he told Lynch to go home and wait. In the meantime, Father Sorin—aware of the fiery patriotism in his student body—praised the cadets for their good spirit but declared that he had no authority to allow boys under twenty-one to enlist without their parents' permission. [11]

Brothers David Lynch, William Lynch and Eugene Lynch and father Timothy Lynch. All of the brothers were officers in the 58th Illinois. William Lynch attended the University of Notre Dame, drilled the school's Continental Cadets and commanded the 58th Illinois during the Civil War. *James William Lynch and Timothy Deichl; photograph previously unpublished.*

William Lynch returned disappointed but not deterred. He left for Chicago and enlisted as a private in Colonel James Mulligan's mostly Irish 23rd Illinois Volunteer Infantry; owing to his experience with the Continental Cadets, Lynch was soon promoted to sergeant major. The regiment left to participate in some of the early battles in Missouri, where after an inspiring but unsuccessful resistance, it surrendered following a siege in Lexington, Missouri, in September 1861. For better or worse, Lynch escaped capture because Mulligan had dispatched him to continue recruiting.

Having missed a second chance to be in the fight, Lynch did not want to miss another. He sought permission from Illinois governor Richard Yates to recruit another regiment. The governor asked for references, and Lynch secured the endorsements of some Indiana statesmen he had met at Notre Dame. These wrote about him that there was "None Better" and that he was a "[g]ood young man; give him a chance." The governor gave his permission, and the newly commissioned Colonel William F. Lynch began recruiting the 58th Illinois Volunteer Infantry. The unit—which counted several other Notre Dame men in its ranks—was mustered into Federal service on Christmas Eve 1861.[12]

Father Gillepsie's guess that only a few students would leave to fight was off the mark. While the exact number is not known, William Lynch was only one of dozens of Notre Dame students who took up arms. "None were braver men or truer patriots," a wartime student wrote years later, adding:

> *Many of them became distinguished; many more took their place in the private ranks, content so that they did their duty well. They were of the unknown, unheralded heroes; whether sick, or wounded, or dead, they were of the mighty majority who finally restored the Union....Notre Dame is honored in her loyal soldier students, who showed, even to the shedding of their blood, how deeply inculcated were the lessons of patriotism which they had received from their Alma Mater.*[13]

SPECIAL ASSIGNMENT

At least three Notre Dame students are known for their Civil War exploits without having ever shouldered a musket: James E. Taylor and brothers William A. and Robert A. Pinkerton. Taylor was born in 1839 in Cincinnati, Ohio. His father, a blacksmith, died when James was only seven, and his mother turned to sewing and boarding tenants to make ends meet. A few years later, she moved the family to northwestern Indiana, and James and his brother Richard both attended Notre Dame from 1850 to 1851. They returned to Cincinnati, and James—only twelve years old—helped the family by working various odd jobs. His passion, though, was in the arts, having shown a talent for drawing and painting at an early age. Indeed, he lost many a job because "his employers would catch him drawing when he should have been working," one Taylor biographer declared.[14]

At the age of fourteen, Taylor submitted some drawings to Nicholas Longworth, a vintner and real estate tycoon and patron of the arts in Cincinnati. Mr. Longworth, impressed with the boy's work, sent him to an art academy in the city, where Taylor, according to his autobiography, "mastered the rudiments of drawing which have since stood [me] in such good stead." Taylor became famous in the region for his panoramas of the American Revolution and the John Brown raid; noted orator Reverend Henry Bellows admired the paintings and brought Taylor to New York to study art. A year later, the Civil War began, and as Taylor wrote, he "laid down the brush...and shouldering his gun at his Country's Call went to the Front" with the 10th New York Volunteer Infantry.[15]

Taylor mustered out as a sergeant at the end of his two years' service, "through which Ordeal he passed Unscathed owing to fortuitous Circumstances," he wrote. In his spare time, he had created a portfolio of sketches of camp life, and rather than reenlist, he showed the sketches to Frank Leslie, publisher of the popular weekly *Frank Leslie's Illustrated Newspaper*. Taylor spent the rest of the war as a "special artist" for Leslie, who counseled Taylor to pay attention to every detail, "even sticks, stones and stumps...regardless of flying bullet and shell." Taylor soon became one of America's best-known artists, and he worked for Leslie for another twenty years before retiring to his studio, where he did freelance work until he died in 1901.[16]

Though they didn't join the army, the Pinkerton brothers shared an exciting war with their father, famed private investigator Allan Pinkerton. Pinkerton was a native of Scotland but had immigrated to the United States in 1842 in his early twenties. A cooper by trade, Pinkerton set up shop in the Chicago suburbs but soon became engaged and admired for his police work. He was attached to the Windy City's police force for a short time before founding Pinkerton's National Detective Agency in

1850 and earning nationwide recognition for foiling and solving railroad and express robberies.

His sons William and Robert were both enrolled during the 1860–61 school year at Notre Dame, where Robert was especially well regarded by his fellow students and the faculty; one of the Holy Cross brothers considered him "the best-natured boy in the [play]yard." Many years later, William wrote to Notre Dame and recalled that he and Robert both had "the kindest remembrances for the dear old place and everyone connected with it." Despite their ages—Robert was only thirteen and William fifteen—the boys were as eager as any of their classmates to enlist. William was allowed to leave his studies and join his father—now chief of the Union army's secret service operation—in the field, while Robert continued his studies at Notre Dame for two more years before joining his father and brother.[17]

William delivered dispatches, escorted agents behind enemy lines, got a bird's-eye view of the Confederate lines in one of Thaddeus Lowe's

William (right) and Robert Pinkerton, sons of famed detective and Union spy Allan Pinkerton, were students at Notre Dame when the war started and helped their father with intelligence operations in the field. *Library of Congress.*

observation balloons and was wounded in the knee by an exploding artillery shell during the Battle of Antietam. In the latter years of the war, Pinkerton and his sons were assigned to the Mississippi Valley, where they investigated contracting and war claims fraud on behalf of the government. Some of William's thrilling undercover operations are related in his father's memoir, *The Spy of the Rebellion*. After the war, the boys became engaged with their father's detective agency and assumed control when the elder Pinkerton died in 1884.

Notre Dame Rebels

Previous accounts of wartime Notre Dame student enlistments have referred primarily to young men joining the Union ranks. As more than 90 percent of the students were from the upper Midwest—Illinois, Indiana, Michigan and Ohio—this is not a surprising phenomenon. Still, even bastions of "Yankeedom" such as Yale, Harvard and Princeton saw a fair number of their students and graduates join the Rebel ranks. So it was with a few young men from Southern states at Notre Dame. At least two students joined the Confederate army.

The first, Michael Quinlan of Wheeling, Virginia (now West Virginia), was born to one of the city's most affluent families. By 1850, however, Michael (and three other siblings) were orphans and living in the home of a local and wealthy merchant. In the 1860 census, Michael is shown as residing in another local home with an estimated personal estate of $6,000, no mean sum for a teenager. Records also show that in 1859 Quinlan was on the roster of a Wheeling militia group called the Virginia State Fencibles.[18]

Quinlan, age eighteen, registered at Notre Dame on August 25, 1860. On October 3, 1860, his account was charged for a pair of military pants (presumably because he had joined the student military company on campus). He was enrolled in a number of classes, including bookkeeping, grammar, fractional arithmetic, German, drawing and dancing. He didn't last long. On December 27, 1860, Quinlan was expelled—for unknown reasons—and sent home to Wheeling.[19]

On May 2, 1861, Quinlan mustered in as a private with Company G—also known as the Shriver Grays—of the 27th Virginia Infantry at Harpers Ferry. His enlistment records show him to be five feet, nine inches tall, with blue eyes, dark hair and a light complexion. The Grays and the 27th Virginia were part of the famed Stonewall Brigade, first under the command of General Thomas J. "Stonewall" Jackson, and saw significant action from First Bull Run—where it suffered more than 140 casualties—through to the surrender at Appomattox, including the Battle of Gettysburg.[20]

In all likelihood, Quinlan never made it to Bull Run and never fired a shot in anger. In June 1861, he was listed as absent and "in arrest at Winchester"—for unknown reasons—but was present on the December 31, 1861 company roll. In spring 1862, he was listed as absent and in the Lynchburg Hospital and then as "absent without leave" until the end of 1862, when he was dropped from the rolls as a deserter. In fact, Quinlan was at the Staunton, Virginia hospital and diagnosed with "valvular disease of the heart and asthma." On December 19, 1862, he was declared unfit for duty, received an official disability discharge and, finally, his back pay of $102.63. Michael Quinlan died on Christmas Day 1863, the local paper noting the cause as "inflammation of the lungs."[21]

Another Notre Dame student who joined the Confederate ranks was Felix Zeringue of New Orleans, Louisiana. Felix enrolled in 1860 and attended Notre Dame until April 21, 1861—just days after the firing on Sumter—when he was given money to go home. After returning home to Orleans Parish, Felix, along with eight other men of the Zeringue clan, enlisted with the 30th Louisiana Infantry, also known as the Sumter Regiment.[22]

Except for a short stint in the hospital, Felix Zeringue was with the 30th Louisiana for the duration and saw some hard fighting, especially late in the war in battles around Atlanta, including the Battle of Ezra Church on July 28, 1864, when the unit (reduced to a battalion) lost its flag and nearly three-fourths of its men were killed or wounded. Felix survived that engagement but was wounded in the leg in the Atlanta campaign. He was captured at the Battle of Nashville, December 17, 1864, and was sent as a prisoner to Camp Douglas in Chicago, Illinois. He left no record of his experiences there, but they must have been hard—thousands of his fellow prisoners perished from disease, starvation and the bitter cold. He was released in New Orleans in July 1865.[23]

Unfortunately, the names of many of the Notre Dame students who enlisted in the early days of the war have been lost to history. Added to that are an untold number of men who had attended or graduated years earlier and enlisted as well. Still, some of them—like Lynch—left a wonderful legacy in their accomplishments or their writings, or both, and their stories are told in these pages.

Chapter 2

FISHERS OF MEN

When you are about to go into battle, the priest shall come forward and say to the soldiers, "Today you are going into battle against your enemies. Be not weakhearted or afraid; be neither alarmed nor frightened by them."

—Deuteronomy 20:2

Chaplains have been a part of military history since Old Testament times. Even the Egyptians and Romans participated in pagan rituals before battles to seek a favorable outcome and to harden the nerves of their legions. Indeed, it is from a once pagan Roman soldier—St. Martin of Tours (AD 316–97)—that we get the word "chaplain." Legend has it that Martin, with his regiment in Gaul, met a nearly naked beggar shivering from the cold and divided his coat into two parts to clothe the poor man. In one version, Martin then had a vision that it was actually Jesus to whom he gave the cloak; in another, he woke to find the cloak miraculously restored.

Martin converted to Christianity and later became the patron saint of France. His cloak—in Latin, *cappa*—now a holy relic, was carried into battle by the Frankish kings. The portable shrine was called the *capella* and its caretaker priest, the *cappellanus*. Over time, all clergy affiliated with military were called *capellani* (or in French, *chapelains*) and, hence, chaplains. Chaplains were officially sanctioned by the medieval church at the Council of Ratisbon in 742, though they were strictly forbidden from bearing arms or fighting. In America, chaplains were with the armies and navies during the American Revolution and in all conflicts since, and they continue to play a crucial role in the welfare of the country's servicemen and women as they live their motto, *Pro Deo et Patria*.

As with so many other aspects of supplying the Union and Confederate armies, the sheer size of the belligerent forces in the Civil War strained the resources of the chaplaincy. By law, only thirty chaplains were allotted to the nineteen regiments of the prewar army; by 1861, the Union army alone had nearly seven hundred regiments under arms. President Lincoln recognized the value of spiritual support in the Northern ranks, and official regulations allowed for one chaplain to be appointed to each regiment, on the vote of the officers. Still, contrary to centuries of military tradition, there was a unique American anticlerical strain, as evidenced in one chaplain's recollection: "Over four hundred voted for a Catholic priest, one hundred and fifty-four, for any kind of a protestant minister; eleven, for a Mormon elder; and three hundred and thirty-five said they could find their way to hell without the assistance of clergy."[24]

In any event, Catholic soldiers were certainly at a disadvantage compared with their Protestant brethren; in 1862, when they represented more than 10 percent of the men in the Union ranks, there were fewer than thirty Catholic chaplains among nearly five hundred then on duty. To meet this need, Father Sorin declared that "Notre Dame...at once thought of providing those Catholic soldiers with the help of their holy religion"; the school would eventually send seven of its priests to serve as chaplains in the armies and hospitals over the course of the war. This was no small sacrifice. America was still a missionary country—especially in the unsettled areas—and the priests that Notre Dame and other religious orders sent strained an already scarce supply of clergy.[25]

The seven—Fathers Paul Gillen, James Dillon, Zepherin Lévêque, Julian Bourget, Joseph Carrier, Peter Cooney and William Corby—did Notre Dame and the Holy Cross community proud, each in his own way. At least two of the priests died during the war while tending to the spiritual needs of wounded and sick soldiers in camps or hospitals; another died shortly after the war from the privations of service. One of the priests was chaplain for only a short time, but in that time he tended to the dying son of one of the war's most famous generals. Two priests, Cooney and Corby, distinguished themselves especially for their bravery. Those two also left the richest personal accounts of their ministry and service, and their singular contributions to the war effort are detailed throughout the book, based on their memoirs and letters.

The Damndest Clergyman I Ever Saw

The first of Notre Dame's priests to go to war as a chaplain was Father Paul E. Gillen. A native of County Donegal, Ireland, Gillen came to the United States in 1840, probably in his late teens (his birth year is unknown), and was engaged across the United States and in Canada as an agent for the *Boston Pilot*, a popular Irish Catholic newspaper. Shortly before the Civil War, he became a priest and entered the Holy Cross community at Notre Dame.

When the war broke out, Father Gillen was on university business in the Northeast. Impressed with the number of Catholic men joining the

Father Paul E. Gillen, CSC.

ranks—and concerned with their spiritual well-being—he appealed for permission to offer his services, and Father Sorin granted the request. Father Gillen arrived in Washington, D.C., on July 20, 1861, on the eve of the First Battle of Bull Run, and immediately began his ministry among the soldiers. Although in his late fifties, Gillen—"a tall, thin, spared old gentleman of clerical appearance"—had seemingly endless energy and did not leave the service until after the surrender at Appomattox.[26]

Father Gillen, in an unconventional approach, did not seek a commission with a particular regiment but instead preferred to roam from unit to unit as needed (a practice that landed him in some hot water later in the war). Given the large compass of his "parish," the energetic priest needed a convenient way to travel. "I felt the great disadvantage of not having a horse," he wrote Father Sorin, and he so appealed to Major General George McClellan. Father Gillen succeeded in getting a horse and ambulance from the quartermaster, but "the officials restricted me to come and show the horse's head at headquarters once a day," which presented its own disadvantages. Besides, he wrote, "the ambulance was designed for the sick and the dead" and was a vehicle that a companion chaplain did not relish, so he paid $100 for a horse, harness and buggy.[27]

Father Gillen was widely known for his new and unique conveyance. "I have got a camp bed similar to the one I left in Notre Dame and also an altar on the same principle with spring feet," he wrote Father Sorin, adding, "I can set it within the frame of the bed and put all in the buggy with candles, candlesticks and all requisites for the Mission." Wherever he stopped at night, Father Gillen could sleep in his own bed, put his altar up quickly in the morning and "proceed from camp to camp as Generalissimo of Chaplains and Missionaries." One officer humorously described Father Gillen's contraption as "a combination of a Plimpton bedstead, a Cathedral, and a restaurant all combined." Still, the officer declared, "No matter whether we were on a march or a scout, Mass was always offered every morning at Father Paul's establishment."[28]

Father Gillen's good standing with the soldiers and officers was marred in late 1861 over rumors of drunkenness. "I have learned with deep affliction that Rev'd [Paul] Edward Gillen…has appeared in a state of intoxication amidst the soldiers among whom he is serving as a volunteer chaplain," wrote Archbishop Kenrick of Baltimore to Father Sorin. Likewise, Bishop James F. Wood of Philadelphia wrote that Gillen had been seen "in a state of brutal intoxication." They also charged that he had "gathered a large sum of money from the soldiers" for his own purpose. Both bishops thought it best that the purportedly wayward priest be called back home. Father Sorin, "surprised" and "grieved" at the scandal, replied and promised to send "another of our fathers to…go to the troops in Washington."[29]

In fact, the rumors were false. In a letter in late November 1861, Archbishop Kenrick declared his satisfaction that "[Father Gillen's] habits are correct." The esteemed prelate attributed his inclination to believe the rumors to "newspaper complaints of the scandalous conduct of volunteer chaplains in that direction," which "increased my apprehension." Actually, Father Gillen acquitted himself with courage on the battlefield. "He would frequently expose himself to great danger in order to administer the rites of the Church to the dying men," one officer recalled. Another officer, impressed that Father Gillen was not afraid of walking alone behind enemy lines after a battle, exclaimed that the chaplain was "one of the damndest venturesome old clergyman I ever saw."[30]

Eventually, General Grant issued an order forbidding civilians (including Father Gillen) and unauthorized vehicles (including Father Gillen's singular buggy) within the army's lines. Determined to continue his ministry, Gillen obtained a commission as chaplain with the 170th New York Infantry, where he continued his work until the end of the war, after which he returned to Notre Dame. He died in 1882.

THE TEMPERANCE REGIMENT

Like Father Gillen, another Notre Dame priest—Father James Dillon—was also in the Northeast on university business in the summer of 1861. While there, he became acquainted with officers who were organizing and recruiting the 63rd New York Volunteer Infantry, which would become part of the famous "Irish Brigade" of the Army of the Potomac. The regiment—like the other core regiments of the brigade—was almost exclusively Catholic, and at the urging of its officers, Father Dillon volunteered to be the regimental chaplain. Father Dillon was "young, but of mature mind, and quite eloquent," a fellow chaplain wrote, adding that he "was impulsive and ardent, and threw his whole soul into any good work he undertook."[31]

By all accounts, Father Dillon—more than any of Notre Dame's priests—took particular care to "guard his boys against the prevailing vices." The worst of these temptations was drunkenness, which was endemic to camp life in the army. In sermons, Father Dillon declared drinking to be the "father of all crimes," especially among the Irish. To foster good behavior among the men, Father Dillon established a "Temperance Society," and hundreds of the men in his regiment joined on the spot. The effects seemed immediately beneficial: attendance at religious service increased and incidents of "camp carousals" decreased. Father Dillon was so pleased that he arranged to distribute medals among the men who had taken the pledge.[32]

Like Father Gillen—indeed, like all of the priests Notre Dame sent to minister to the soldiers—Father Dillon was cool under fire. "Father Dillon was always ready to take part in a skirmish or a ride through the enemy's country," a brigade surgeon remembered. Indeed, in one instance, Father Dillon even managed to bring order out of chaos in the heat of battle (albeit "outstepping the lines of his proper duty") when he rallied the regiment at the Battle of Malvern Hill on July 1, 1862. The regiment was under fire, and its officers were *hors du combat*. There was great confusion as to whom they should obey. One of the men exclaimed, "This is Father Dillon's regiment!" A chorus joined in, yelling, "Yes, yes! Give us Father Dillon!" The good chaplain came forward, assured the soldiers that he would remain with them and then calmly passed among the ranks, informing the men that they should obey the officer now in command.[33]

Father Dillon was not even thirty years old when he joined the army; almost exactly a year later, he was honorably discharged. "Against the advice of the best army physicians he remained in the army much longer than he should have," Father Sorin wrote a year later, explaining that exposure in the camps had aggravated lung problems that Father Dillon had endured since his youth. "He went to Europe, but returned after twelve months in about the same state of health," Father Sorin continued, adding that doctors had advised Father Dillon to travel to California and that "it will take a year to pronounce on the improvement in his health." Unfortunately, the relief did not come, and Father Dillon died of complications of his lung troubles in 1870.[34]

Two other Notre Dame priests died during the war while serving as chaplains. In 1861, Father Sorin kept good his promise, made in response to the (untrue) rumors of Father Gillen's intoxication, to send another priest to minister to the Catholic troops; that priest was Father Zepherin Joseph Lévêque, a Canadian by birth. While as zealous as Father Gillen,

Father Lévêque was also sickly and did not serve for long. On February 13, 1862—just a few months after arriving—he fell ill and died while visiting a fellow priest in New Jersey. Like Father Gillen, Father Lévêque did not seem to have a commission with a particular regiment, although an obituary in the *New York Herald* stated that "the members of Company K, Twelfth Regiment, New York State Militia" were invited to attend the funeral.[35]

Another priest, Father Julian Prosper Bourget, had come to Notre Dame from the Holy Cross Mother House in France in early 1862. At Father Sorin's suggestion, Father Bourget left for the military hospital at Mound City, Illinois, where he cared for many wounded and dying soldiers. Unfortunately, his stay—like Father Lévêque's—was not long. Father Bourget contracted malaria and died at the hospital on June 12, 1862.

GENIUS, INTERRUPTED

Father Joseph C. Carrier was born in France in 1833, the youngest of ten children in a respected and wealthy family. He received his early education under the care of a private tutor before attending the College of Belley, where he excelled in all of his studies but especially in science and mathematics. Indeed, while only in his late teens, he was appointed professor of natural philosophy (physics) at a small college in Geneva, Switzerland. In 1855, he came to America and decided to enter the priesthood. His patron—the bishop of St. Paul, Minnesota—had high hopes for establishing a religious order and college in his part of the country and thought that the young scholar would be an ideal choice to lead both.

Unfortunately, the bishop died before he or his protégé could act on the plan. Instead, Carrier entered the Holy Cross community at Notre Dame, where he was ordained a priest in early 1861. In May 1863, Father Carrier was serving as a professor of Latin and Greek at the university, as well as a pastor of the church in nearby South Bend, when Father Sorin told him to be ready to leave at a moment's notice to join General Ulysses S. Grant's army as a chaplain. Within days, Father Carrier bid farewell to his students and parishioners and set out for Mississippi, where he was commissioned as chaplain of the 6th Missouri Infantry Regiment. In fact, his ministry extended to all of Grant's army.

By all accounts, Father Carrier was as comfortable among the leading generals of the army as he was among the common soldier. When he met

Father Joseph C. Carrier, CSC. *Priests of Holy Cross, Indiana Province Archives Center.*

Grant for the first time, the general asked if he was a professor. "Yes," Father Carrier replied, "I have been years in the college of Notre Dame and am still attached to it." The general then declared, "You will find that the life of a soldier is quite different from that of a professor and that our tents are not so comfortable as the halls of a college." The good priest replied, "I understood that before I left Notre Dame, I did not expect to find in the soldiers' camp all the comforts, the conveniences, and ease of home." Grant expressed his happiness that Father Carrier had joined his army, and the two men then discussed the progress of the siege at Vicksburg.[36]

While all of Notre Dame's priests may have steeled themselves for the vagaries of camp life, they must have been less prepared for the constant threat and presence of death. The bookish Father Carrier seemed to be the most sensitive to this grim reality. In advance of the great "Vicksburg mine" explosion on June 25, 1863, Father Carrier witnessed a Union soldier being killed by a Confederate sniper. Father Carrier was "much moved by the terrible sudden…death of the soldier" and "sat at the foot of the tree." Rather than watch the historic detonation, as his fellow officers were doing, Father Carrier "fell into a deep and irrepressible reverie," left the scene, went back to camp "and threw himself on his cot." To his credit, Father Carrier returned to the lines and ministered to some of the soldiers wounded in the post-explosion charge.[37]

Before the end of the year, Father Carrier was called back to Notre Dame, where he began to place the school's scientific program on a firm foundation. In 1866, he spent several months in Paris collecting laboratory apparatus and specimens for the university's museum of natural history. His greatest coup was securing a six-inch telescope as a gift from Emperor Napoleon III. Father Carrier was the longtime curator of the museum and professor of chemistry and physics. He was eventually assigned as a professor at St. Laurent College, near Montreal, and expertly tended the museum there until his death in 1904.

QUITE A MILITARY APPEARANCE

Father Peter P. Cooney was born in 1822 in County Roscommon, Ireland. When Cooney was five years old, his family came to the United States and settled near Monroe, Michigan, where he attended the local public schools. Peter Cooney was almost thirty years old when he came to Notre Dame as a student in 1850. After graduation, he taught for some time at a country school. He then decided that he was called to the priesthood and joined the Holy Cross community at Notre Dame, where he was ordained in 1859. His first appointment was at the University of St. Mary's of the Lake near Chicago, then under the direction of the Congregation of Holy Cross.

Father Cooney was preparing to join other priests in mission work across the United States when the Civil War broke out. In the fall of 1861, Indiana governor Oliver P. Morton asked Father Sorin for priests to minister to the Catholics in the regiments that the state was sending to the rapidly growing Union armies. Father Cooney was eager to go and was appointed chaplain to the 35th Indiana Volunteer Infantry—also known as the state's "First Irish" regiment—in October 1861.

Soon after joining his regiment, Father Cooney began writing letters, mainly to his brother, Owen, at home in Michigan. These

Father Peter P. Cooney,
CSC. *Priests of Holy
Cross, Indiana Province
Archives Center.*

letters give wonderful firsthand testimony to his activities as a chaplain, the role his regiment played in some major battles of the war and the character—especially the religious habits—of some important military personalities of the war, especially General William Rosecrans.

More than any of Notre Dame's priests, Father Cooney took to military life—including the uniform and accoutrements—with great zeal. In one of his first letters home, he described his horse ("the finest in the regiment") and his uniform, which he declared "[gives] me quite a military appearance," adding:

> *There are gold chords down the sides of my pants and on my shoulders there are black velvet pieces about four inches long and two inches wide,*

surrounded with gold lace in the shape C+N. The Cross in the center is embroidered with gold thread. The CN, the first and last letters of the word "chaplain," are embroidered with gold also. The buttons on my coat are bright black gutta percha buttons and around my hat I wear a gold band with gold tassels. The whole makes a very appropriate uniform for a priest. The Bishop of Louisville was very well pleased with it a few days ago when I went to see him. I wear my Roman collar as before. Around my waist I wear a blue silk sash about five inches wide with tassels. The shoulder pieces were embroidered by the sisters.[38]

Father Cooney and the 35th Indiana did not see significant action until late in 1862, but the men—and their chaplain—would be in the thick of it.

Unflinching Devotion

Few of Notre Dame's wartime chaplains—indeed, few among all the chaplains of the Civil War—have received as much attention as Father William Corby. Corby was born in Detroit, Michigan. His father, Daniel Corby—an adept real estate dealer and a devout Catholic—was a native Irishman who had come to Michigan through Canada, where he had married. As a teenager, William had worked with his father and seemed destined for a career in business himself. In reality, he very much wanted to attend college and study for the priesthood. To that end, Daniel sent William and his two younger brothers to Notre Dame, where William quickly became a favorite of Father Sorin. He was ordained in 1860 and within the year had assumed important responsibilities at the college.

In the fall of 1861, Father Dillon—already stretched in the service of the mostly Catholic Irish Brigade—asked Father Sorin to send Father Corby to assist him. Father Corby left Chicago bound for Washington, D.C., on the Pittsburgh & Fort Wayne Railway. "On my journey I thought over the problems of the future," he remembered years later; "the chances of ever returning to my bright, prosperous college home, of the dear ones I left behind." Having never been east before, Father Corby confessed that he "felt alone…strange, in new lands among new people." Once he arrived, though, Father Corby was among old friends. He soon reunited with Fathers Dillon and Gillen and found his own "congregation" among the men of the 88th New York Infantry.[39]

Taken in the summer of 1862 at Harrison's Landing, Virginia. *Back row, left to right*: Father Patrick Dillon, CSC, and an unidentified man. Front row, left to right: unidentified man and chaplains Father James Dillon, CSC, and Father William Corby, CSC. *Library of Congress.*

Of his first winter in camp, Father Corby explained, with characteristic humor, that he and his fellow chaplains "spent our time in much the same way as parish priests do, except in this—we had no old women to bother us, or pew rent to collect." He spent the next three years among the men of the Irish Brigade and wrote of his experiences in a wonderful book, *Memoirs of Chaplain Life*. For their part, the soldiers were happy to have him; of Father Corby, one officer wrote that he was "a man whose courage was not surpassed by the bravest soldier of our armies, whose unflinching devotion on the march, in camp and under fire made him eminent."[40]

Chapter 3

A FLOCK OF WHITE DOVES

Mother Angela of St. Mary's Academy has come with thirty nurses—a flock of white doves—to nurse in the hospitals, where the stillness is like the silence of death…When [laywomen] get tired, they go home, but the Sisters of the Holy Cross live among the patients without thought of avoiding contagion by flight.
—Letter, Mrs. Susan E. Wallace, wife of General Lew Wallace, to her mother, December 18, 1861

Four years of fighting during the American Civil War left more than 600,000 soldiers dead, two-thirds of whom succumbed to diseases rather than shot, sword or shell. More important from a medical standpoint is that many times that number were left wounded or sick and required care. From the outset, it was clear that the medical departments of both belligerents were unprepared for the task ahead of them—the Confederate effort had to be built from scratch, and the Union medical department started with a small contingent of surgeons and "old school" leadership more concerned with budgets and politics and less with innovations that would be required to manage the crisis.

It is one of the great success stories of the Civil War that military hospital conditions significantly improved with time. Still, the primary care of the great number of sick and wounded taxed the limits of regimental and hospital surgeons, who needed support for other activities such as providing clean dressings, clothing and bedding; distributing medicines; cooking palatable and nutritious food; and offering moral support—in other words, the basic functions of nursing. Unfortunately, professional nursing was still in its infancy in the United States; most medical care was tendered in the home rather than in hospitals, and nursing traditions were passed from generation to generation.

At first, invalids, prisoners or soldiers on special detail were assigned as nurses, but they generally lacked the skills—or even the desire—to perform their duties. Laywomen stepped in by the thousands to fill the void but were not always welcome. One surgeon wrote, "Our women appear to have become almost wild on the subject of hospital nursing. We honor them for their sympathy and humanity. Nevertheless…they, with the best intentions in the world, are frequently a useless annoyance." While this surgeon's main complaint was the limitation of "delicate refined women," another surgeon—John H. Brinton—found the ladies' demands to be unreasonable:

> They did not wish much…"simply a room, a bed, a looking glass, someone to get their meals and do little things for them," and they would nurse the "sick boys of our gallant Union Army." Can you fancy…a dozen old hags, for that is what they were…surrounding a bewildered hospital surgeon, each one clamorous for her little wants?…In short this female nurse business was a great trial to all the men concerned, and to me…soon became intolerable.[41]

In the vacuum created by incompetent men and bothersome laywomen, the surgeons found a welcome solution in the sisters of Catholic religious orders, whose traditions and vows of obedience, poverty, discipline and labor made them ideal candidates for wartime nursing. Some of the orders—especially the Sisters of Charity—operated several hospitals in the prewar years and were able to supply an approximation of professionally trained nurses. Other sisters gained experience in orphanages and schools. By the end of the war, more than six hundred Catholic sisters from more than twenty communities and twelve different orders served as nurses during the war.

The Sisters of the Holy Cross of Notre Dame, Indiana, formed one of the largest cadres of sister-nurses, with more than sixty women serving in army hospitals in Illinois, Kentucky, Tennessee, Missouri and the nation's capital city; they also served on floating hospitals plying the Mississippi River. They set a high standard in their care for the sick and wounded, and though they began the war as a teaching order, their experiences during the Civil War allowed them to expand their mission to healthcare, a ministry that exists to this day.

THE CALL

The call for the Holy Cross sisters to serve as nurses came on the evening of October 21, 1861, when a horseman galloped to the campus of Notre Dame carrying an urgent request for Father Sorin. Sorin read the message to himself and then, by the light of his lantern, walked over to St. Mary's Academy. Once there, he asked for Mother Angela and read her the message. Within hours, she and five companions were bound by train for southern Illinois. The next day, Father Sorin wrote a letter to the sisters explaining the night's events:

> *A most honorable call has been made on your community by the first Magistrate in our state* [Governor Oliver P. Morton] *asking for twelve sisters to go and attend the sick, the wounded and the dying soldiers...wherever there is a pain to soothe, a pang to relieve, a bleeding heart or limb to treat or dress, there is a field for us to enter...Such is the field now opened by the calamity of our land...A little band of devoted sisters, ministering like angels amidst the soldiery, will do away with prejudices and show the beauty and resources of* [our faith] *to support man in all possible trials.*[42]

Mother Angela and her "little army" arrived in Cairo, Illinois, where they reported to General Ulysses S. Grant, who had his headquarters in the city. Sister Magdalene Kieran, a member of the small band, remembered meeting the famous general:

> [He] *shook hands most heartily with each Sister. Over the hand of Mother Angela he bent with the chivalry of a soldier worthy of leading a host to victory. Looking at his visitor with a kindly smile, he said: "Mother Angela, I am very glad indeed to have you and your Sisters with us."...* [T]*he general asked Mother Angela if she and her companion nurses could be ready to report for duty that night at the military hospital in Paducah* [Kentucky]... [She replied] *that he had but to express a wish and it would be obeyed at once.*[43]

The sisters left right away and arrived in Paducah that evening, where they met General Lew Wallace (whose request for sister-nurses had prompted the governor's message to Father Sorin), who commanded a brigade and its three hospitals in the area. The surgeons were characteristically dubious of having women in their wards, but they were soon impressed with Mother Angela, whom General Grant had spoken of as "a woman of rare charm of manner, unusual ability, and exceptional executive talents." She reorganized the wards "with almost military precision," and the sisters scrubbed the floors free of blood, put fresh linen on the beds, bathed the sick and prepared an appetizing and nutritious diet in the kitchen.[44]

In mid-December 1861, Mother Angela returned to St. Mary's to gather another group of sisters and then headed back to Cairo, where she left Sister Augusta in charge of an army hospital known as "The Bulletin" (the sisters, finding the moniker cheerless, renamed it "St. John's"). Sister Paula Casey remembered her first look at the hospital:

A fearful sight met our gaze. Every room on the first floor was strewn with human legs and arms…Some of the wards resembled a slaughterhouse, the walls were so splattered with blood…Sr. Isidore and I cried with horror. Sr. Augusta looked pityingly at us, but said—"Now stop; you are here and must put your heart and soul into the work. Pin up your habits; we will get three buckets of water and three brooms and begin by washing the walls and then the floors."

Sister Augusta asked the surgeon in charge to detail some men to remove the limbs and to secure the buckets and mops; the sisters went to work. "The first few nights we had no beds," Sister Paula added, "but we were so tired that we slept soundly on the floor."[45]

The Holy Cross sister-nurses in Paducah and Cairo quickly earned an admirable reputation for both their service and their administrative abilities. Mary Livermore, a renowned abolitionist and women's suffragette, inspected the Cairo hospital on behalf of the United States Sanitary Commission and recalled, "The 'Sisters of the Holy Cross' were employed as nurses, one or more to each ward. Here were order, comfort, cleanliness, and good nursing." Owing to that reputation, Mother Angela soon received orders to provide another corps of sisters to take charge of a hospital in Kentucky and for more sisters still in Tennessee, Missouri and Washington, D.C. By the end of the war, Holy Cross sister-nurses were serving in at least ten hospitals.[46]

Clean and Sweet

It was at the Union army hospital in Mound City, Illinois, where most of the Holy Cross sisters would serve. The call for the sisters to Mound City came from no less than Dr. John H. Brinton, the very man who had referred to the legion of lay female nurses as "old hags." In his memoirs, he wrote:

> *In answer to my request to the Catholic authorities of…South Bend, Indiana, a number of sisters were sent down to act as nurses in the hospital. These sent were from a teaching and not from a nursing order, but in a short time they adapted themselves admirably to their duties…I remember their black and white dresses, and I remember also, that when I asked the Mother, who accompanied them, what accommodation they required, the answer was, "One room, Doctor," and there were in all, I think, fourteen or fifteen of them. So I procured good nurses for my sick and…*[they] *gained by the change.*[47]

The Mound City hospital was a large unfinished complex of about two dozen warehouses. The sisters designated each warehouse as a ward and assigned a letter of the alphabet to each. While the wards were supposed to accommodate only 20 to 30 men each, at times—especially after a battle—there were as many as 1,400 patients under treatment, many of the sick being prisoners of war.

"The buildings [at Mound City] were…very crude," Sister Ferdinand recalled, "and the boards on the floor were in places separated very widely." The poor flooring had some grim effects on the sisters; Sister Anthony recalled that while sleeping in the small dormitory below the wards, the sisters "would be awakened by the blood and pus…dripping onto their beds through the cracks in the ceiling and floor above them." Sister Francis de Sales O'Neil remembered a similar scene after the Battle of Fort Donelson in early 1862:

> *Mother Angela was assisting Doctor Franklin with a difficult operation, the precise accuracy of which would determine the life or death of a soldier. A little chloroform had to suffice to dull the agony of the probing. Both surgeon and assistant leaned intently over the patient. Suddenly a red drop fell on Mother Angela's white coif. Another and still another fell until a small stream was seeping through the ceiling. But true to her Celtic ancestry Mother Angela remained motionless, with thoughts*

Left: The Mound City, Illinois warehouse used as a hospital and staffed by the Sisters of the Holy Cross.

Below: The U.S. Hospital at Mound City, Illinois, staffed by the Sisters of the Holy Cross. *Naval Historical Center.*

concentrated on the delicate surgery. At last the final stitch was taken; two heads rose simultaneously. Not until then did the doctor realize that a crimson rivulet from the floor above had fallen steadily upon our Mother's devoted head, bathing coif, face, and shoulders in blood.[48]

As she had at Cairo, Mary Livermore inspected the hospital at Mound City and had equal praise for the Holy Cross sisters' work:

The Mound City Hospital was considered the best military hospital in the United States...The most thorough system was maintained in every department. There were an exact time and place for everything...A Shaker-like cleanliness and sweetness of atmosphere pervaded the various wards, the sheets and pillows were of immaculate whiteness, and the patients who were convalescing were cheerful and contented. The "Sisters of the Holy Cross" were employed as nurses, and by their skill, quietness, gentleness, and tenderness, were invaluable in the sick-wards. Every patient gave hearty testimony to the kindness and skill of the "Sisters."[49]

Unfortunately, just as Father Sorin had lost two of the priests he had sent as chaplains to disease in 1862, so too did Mother Angela lose two of her sister-nurses that year, both at Mound City. The first, Sister Fidelis, had come to the Mound City hospital in November 1861 and was given charge of the clothes room, where she gave out clean clothes and bedding. In the spring of 1862, the already frail sister contracted a serious cold and died on Good Friday. The Mound City hospital had been subject to heavy rains that spring, and Sister Paula—who was with Sister Fidelis when she died—remembered, "as her lifeless body lay on her cot, the water rose rapidly...A soldier brought her coffin in a skiff, and we placed her body on it; it was then rowed through the woods to the Railroad Station, to meet the train for Chicago en route to St. Mary's." Another nurse, Sister Elise, died of illness a few months later.[50]

PIONEERS

On Christmas Eve 1862, three Holy Cross sister-nurses boarded the USS *Red Rover*, the navy's first floating hospital ship. According to the navy's own official history, the women represented another important first: "[They] may truly be said to be the pioneers or forerunners of the United States Navy Nurse Corps as they were the first female nurses carried on board a United States Navy Hospital Ship."[51]

Built in Cape Girardeau, Missouri, in 1859, the *Red Rover* began its riverine life as a commercial side-wheel steamer. In late 1861, the Confederacy bought the steamer in New Orleans, renamed it CSS *Red Rover* and used it as an unarmed barracks for soldiers and sailors assigned to a nearby floating artillery battery. In early 1862, the *Red Rover* made its way up the Mississippi River but was abandoned a month after being damaged in a Union naval bombardment. Federals captured the ship, and following on-the-spot repairs, the steamer made its way to St. Louis, where the newly christened USS *Red Rover* was refitted as a floating hospital for the Western Gunboat Flotilla.

Mother Angela happily offered her sisters as nurses on the unique floating hospital, and when the *Red Rover* was transferred to the navy in late 1862, she sent Sister Veronica Moran, Sister Adela Reilly and Sister Callista Pointan from the Mound City hospital for service on the steamer. They were joined by two African American women, who served under their direction. Other Holy Cross sisters also served on the steamer, but Sister Veronica and Sister Adela served continuously until November 1865. The sister-nurses earned fifty cents per day (ten cents more than their counterparts in the army), though they were subject to the same irregular pay as soldiers and sailors (in a hospital account book, Mother Angela chided: "The paymaster is generally very tardy, leaving an interval of several months between his appearances").[52]

The *Red Rover* set out on December 29, 1862, leaving Mound City and passing down the river toward Memphis, then Helena, Arkansas, and finally to the Yazoo River, where it received orders to guard the mouth of the White River while the flotilla bombarded Arkansas Post (Fort Hindman), Arkansas, and transported troops to storm the fort; the wounded were transferred to the *Red Rover* after the successful assault. Even though the *Red Rover* was a hospital ship, the steamer was armed and sometimes a target. On January 21, 1863, Rebel artillery fired on the *Red Rover*, and two shots entered the hospital. Sister Adela recalled that during the Vicksburg campaign, the *Red Rover* "was near enough to hear the firing and also to see the boats running the blockade."[53]

The USS *Red Rover* and its Holy Cross sister-nurses were featured in a handsome series of engravings in the May 9, 1863 issue of *Harper's Weekly*. The caption declared:

> *This institution…is under the charge of Surgeon George H. Bixby and Dr. Hopkins, and is an untold comfort to our sick or wounded sailors. The sketch shows the main ward, in which are accommodations for over two hundred patients. The Sister is one of those good women whose angelic services have been sung by poets and breathed by grateful convalescents all the world over. The convalescents are placed in a ward for their sole use, where they smoke, read, and generally enjoy themselves. The boat itself, a clean, roomy craft, is under the command of a gallant old sailor.*[54]

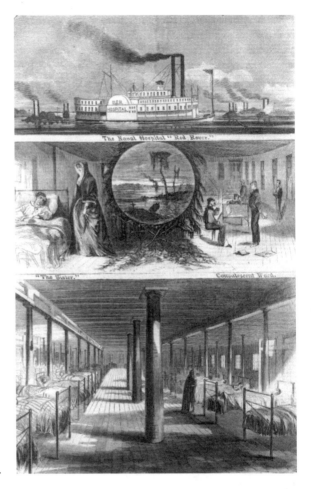

The Sisters of the Holy Cross on the USS *Red Rover* floating hospital ship. *Harper's Weekly*, May 9, 1863.

In addition to being a generous and contemporary tribute, the engravings are thought to be the only wartime depictions of the Holy Cross sister-nurses in action.

CHALLENGES AND TRIUMPHS

Despite the praise of Surgeon Brinton, Mary Livermore and General Grant, not everyone shared their views, and the sister-nurses were subject to considerable prejudice owing to their faith, their ethnicity or both. Sometimes the prejudice was innocent; even Mary Livermore recalled that she "often sympathized with some of the sick men who frequently expressed a wish for a reform in the 'headgear' of the 'Sisters,'" adding that one of the "irreverent critics" declared that their habits were "a cross between a white sun-bonnet and a broken-down umbrella."[55]

Generally, the prejudice was more insidious; curiously, some of the fiercest critics were women further emboldened by jealousy at the praise heaped on the sisters by the medical community. Chief among the detractors was Dorothea Dix, superintendent of army nurses. Politically aligned with nativists and anti-Catholics, Dix refused to employ Catholic sisters and enjoined her subordinates to avoid them as well. Other influential women cruelly stated that Catholic sisters were not fit to be nurses due to their "coldness"; Abby Hopper Gibbons wrote that the sisters were "the machinery of an Institution and do not minster to the broken down in spirit." Still, for every Dix and Gibbons there was a Livermore, who declared, "If I had ever felt prejudice against these 'Sisters' as nurses, my experience with them during the war would have dissipated it entirely. The world has known no nobler and no more heroic women."[56]

"We were not prepared as nurses," Sister Augusta Anderson recalled, "but our hearts made our hands willing and our sympathy ready, and so with God's help, we did much towards alleviating the dreadful suffering." Though, as Sister Augusta attested, the Sisters of the Holy Cross started the war as a teaching order, their experience allowed them to expand their postwar mission. While they continued their educational ministry and founded more than one hundred academies, schools and colleges after the war, they also started a system of Holy Cross hospitals, beginning in Cairo, Illinois, in 1867; they now administer one of the largest Catholic healthcare systems in the country.[57]

Seemingly lost in the Holy Cross sisters' tales of four years of tender ministrations to the sick and dying is the story of the strong woman who led the original band after the first call in October 1861: Mother Angela. The lack of a personal account belies her tireless activity. She might be found scrubbing floors or assisting in surgery, but even behind the scenes Mother Angela was exercising her considerable influence and executive abilities by placing trusted subordinates in charge of other hospitals and writing friends, strangers, officers and politicians for supplies. Perhaps, though, it was her example of confidence and humility that did the most good. "There are some people who can inspire others to do what ordinarily speaking is impossible; Mother Angela was one of these," one sister wrote. "Her faith and courage never recognized limitations; hence the nature, the magnitude of her achievements and those of her Sisters."[58]

Chapter 4

HURLED INTO TARTARUS

'Twas needful, Sherman said, that Shiloh's shock
Of arms should come, when men unflinching stood,
E'en to the shedding of the warm, red blood.
—*"Aristos," poem by Timothy E. Howard*

A t the end of three months…peace was as far away as it had been at the beginning, and the terror that haunted the land was the same as that inspired by the first cannon-fire in the harbor of Charleston," wrote Father Sorin of the widespread yet misplaced optimism that the Civil War would be over in ninety days. "We all became conversant in the idea of warfare," he added. "Never before had the [American] public had to puzzle out who would stand up and who would fall in the face of a tempest like this."[59]

Of the university's role in the war, Father Sorin justly concluded that "the year 1862 was for several reasons a memorable one in the annals of the Congregation of Holy Cross in the United States" for "the sending of new chaplains and of a still larger number of Sisters to the army; their successes, their dangers, their trials, the deaths taking place in their ranks." The same held true of the "dangers, trials and deaths" in the ranks of Notre Dame's student-soldiers, for 1862 would prove to be particularly devastating in that regard.[60]

BAPTISM OF FIRE

By early February 1862, Colonel William Lynch had completed filling the ranks of the 58th Illinois Volunteer Infantry. The regiment—almost nine hundred strong—left Chicago on February 11 by rail for Cairo, Illinois, where it was furnished with arms, albeit faulty hand-me-downs. It then received orders to leave immediately on river transports bound for the vicinity of Fort Donelson, built by the Confederates to guard the Cumberland River's approach to Tennessee. The 58th Illinois was not long in "seeing the elephant"; it was subjected to artillery fire from the fort soon after arriving and participated in an important assault on the following day. The adjutant general's report declared that the conduct of Lynch and his unit "was remarkable; raw men…behaved as well as veterans of a hundred battles."[61]

The Confederate garrison at Fort Donelson surrendered on February 16. After several more weeks of drilling and marching deeper into Tennessee, Lynch and his regiment arrived at Pittsburgh Landing on the western bank of the Tennessee River in late March, near a small log church named Shiloh, where they joined General Grant's army. Early on the morning of April 6, Confederate forces under Generals Albert S. Johnston and P.G.T. Beauregard launched a surprise attack on the Union army at the landing. Soon after hearing the cannon and rifle fire of the growing battle, the 58th Illinois was ordered to fall in.

The regiment formed in a line of battle and marched to meet the enemy, suffering a "galling cross-fire of two field batteries and heavy infantry fire of several regiments of the enemy," which were advancing on its front. Owing to the surprise attack and panic in some of the Union regiments, the 58th Illinois and its sister regiments found themselves surrounded. "Colonel Lynch arose in his saddle and gave the order to 'cut their way through,'" an officer declared in the regiment's official report. White flags were seen amidst Union regiments to the left and rear of the 58th Illinois, and "then a white flag was seen upon the extreme right of our line, which [Colonel Lynch] seeing rode up and with his sword struck it to the ground," the report continued.[62]

By then it was too late. "Let me tell you in a few words that but *few* Regiments fought better than ours," a soldier in the 58th Illinois wrote home, "and that after many of our brave boys had fallen in defence of our beloved banner…we finally had to give ourselves up as prisoners." More than two hundred men in the 58th Illinois—including Colonel

Lynch—were taken prisoner. The next day, the Union army launched a surprise counterattack and won the battle, the bloodiest in American history up to that time.[63]

Under guard, the captives marched twenty miles to Corinth, Mississippi, in a heavy rain on bad roads and with nothing to eat. After another week on foot, by rail and by steamer, the prisoners arrived at Montgomery, Alabama, where they were lodged in a cotton warehouse. Among the prisoners from the 58th Illinois was Notre Dame student-soldier John C. Lonergan. A native of Batavia, Illinois, he attended Notre Dame from 1855 to 1857 and again from 1859 to 1861, where—among other activities and studies—he was vice-president of the Dramatic Society. Lonergan mustered in with the regiment as a first lieutenant in Company H on February 7, 1862, only days before the regiment shipped out for Fort Donelson. He was wounded during the Battle of Shiloh on April 6 and taken to Montgomery, where he was kept a prisoner until he died of his wounds on May 28, 1862, adding to the growing roll of Notre Dame men and women who gave their lives that spring.

THE WARRIOR POET

Also on the front lines at the Battle of Shiloh was another Notre Dame student-soldier, Timothy E. Howard. Howard was born near Ann Arbor, Michigan, in 1837. He farmed with his father and received no formal schooling until his late teens. He then attended the University of Michigan for a year before returning home to take care of family affairs, his father having died several years earlier. He taught at a local public school for two years, but his "aspiring mind urg[ed] him to seek a higher degree of culture than it had as yet attained," and he thus entered Notre Dame in 1859 to finish his college studies.[64]

In early 1862, Howard enlisted as a private in the 12th Michigan Infantry. The regiment left its home state only three weeks before the Battle of Shiloh. Advance elements of the unit met the enemy early on the morning of April 6 and were engaged in heavy fighting until late that afternoon, losing more than two hundred men killed, wounded or captured. In the maelstrom, Howard was struck in his neck, the bullet only narrowly missing his jugular vein and also severing some of the tendons in his left arm. He was taken by boat to the Marine Hospital in Evansville, Indiana, where he lay for months, recuperating from the wound.

Howard was also an aspiring poet and published a small volume, *Musings and Memories*, many years after the war. Among the poems in his collection was "Convalescent," in which he described the Battle of Shiloh and his recovery:

Through the open hall door comes a balm to my pain;
For the fresh winds of morning are fanning my brain;
And hilarity, borne from the groups on the porch,
Tells the wounded and dying there's joy in the world;
As there will be while life has a spark in his torch,
Though ten thousand an hour were to Tartarus hurled.

Ah, now I can see them. Two sit on the step;
And one leans by a column; one plucks at the nep

And some are more boisterous, telling of fight,
And the way that we put the bold foemen to flight.

So the brave, mellow lads while away the bright morn;
And their stories recounting, their deeds are new born

And I am better, too, at length.
Kind heaven daily gives me strength;
And now I long to tread the grass,
To look upon the trees and skies,
To jostle people as they pass,
And catch the friendship of their eyes.

And I? Nay, then, I'll not repine;
But pain shall still my soul refine;
Though long, so long, this cot I keep,
With bandaged wound, and feverish sleep,

Yes, I am thankful. Maimed and dead
Have rested here, on many a bed;
But life and limb to me are spared,
And faithful hands for me have cared.

The lengthened miles before me lie,
Where the rushing train full soon shall hie.

And I shall lift the dear old latch,
Where glistening eyes for me do watch;
And I shall stand in the open door,
Where welcome waits me, o'er and o'er.[65]

Howard was discharged late that summer and returned to Notre Dame that fall, "where welcome waited him." He enjoyed a long career as a professor of English and rhetoric at the university. He also became active in local politics, serving on the city council and as county clerk. Ever the student, Howard studied law while at Notre Dame and became city attorney of South Bend and then county attorney and state senator before taking a seat as a justice on the Indiana Supreme Court. One historian paid Howard a high compliment, calling him "the consummate Notre Dame man."[66]

THE BATTLE IS OVER...WE ARE SAFE

"On March 5, 1862, general orders were given to 'strike tents' and 'march!'" Father Corby wrote years later as he remembered the day that he, Father Dillon and the Irish Brigade departed from their camp in Virginia and set out on their first campaign. The spring was spent on foot as they marched and by water as they steamed on transports to the Virginia peninsula. After an ill-fated siege at Yorktown, the Confederate army slipped away, and the Union army chased the enemy to the outskirts of the Confederate capital of Richmond, where on May 31, 1862, the armies engaged in the Battle of Fair Oaks. That night, Father Corby and the Irish Brigade reached the battlefield and awoke the next morning to find themselves among the dead and wounded from the previous day's fight. "The impression made on my mind then...is still as fresh as if it were only yesterday," Father Corby wrote of the scene many years later.[67]

The next day, Father Corby witnessed his first battle; of the fury he wrote that it seemed "hell had opened its gates and let loose hundreds of thousands of demons, 'shapes hot from Tartarus,' whose...single aim was destruction." In his official report, Brigadier General Thomas F. Meagher praised the brigade's chaplains for "the courage and the heart with which [they]...stood by their charge in the hour of danger and consoled those who fell."[68]

Had they read newspaper reports of the battle, Father Sorin and the community at Notre Dame would have been justly worried over the fate of the priests they had sent off to war. Father Corby recalled how he put their fears to rest:

> *Just after the battle of Fair Oaks, I wished to send word home to Notre Dame. I had no paper, but, after much searching, I found an old envelope, which had no paste or mucilage to fasten it. I found a stamp, however, and on the inside of the envelope I wrote: "The battle is over, and we are safe." I sealed the letter by pasting the stamp on the laps of the envelope. This I addressed to my dear sister, who handed it to Very Rev. E. Sorin, then the President of Notre Dame. He was so pleased with the real war-like message that he had it read in public to the faculty and students of the university.*[69]

Still, microbes killed twice as many soldiers as bullets during the Civil War, and Notre Dame had already lost two chaplains and two sisters to disease; it might have lost Father Corby to malaria as well were it not for quick action by his friends and the care of sister-nurses. On June 17, 1862, following the Battle of Fair Oaks, Father Corby recalled that he felt "very queerly," but his fellow chaplains and other officers told him the "trouble came from imagination" and from "seeing so many sick and dying." Two days later, however, Father Corby "reeled and fell to the ground." Father Dillon quickly got Father Corby onto a transport bound for Washington and a proper hospital. "I lay insensible with a burning fever for three days," Father Corby recalled, but owing to the tender ministrations of the Sisters of Charity, he was soon well.[70]

Father Corby returned to camp a few weeks later and accompanied his regiment "night and day, in heat and cold, in sunshine and rain; marching and counter-marching in Virginia, Pennsylvania, and Maryland, hundreds if not thousands of miles." Over the course of the next months, he witnessed some of the most sanguinary fights of the war, including the Battles of the Seven Days and Antietam and the Irish Brigade's heroic charge on Confederate breastworks at the Battle of Fredericksburg, where he watched as the men of the brigade "melted away before the grape and canister, and the tens of thousands of muskets." When he said Mass the following morning, Father Corby recalled that "I had a very small congregation compared with former ones...All of us were sad, very sad."[71]

Always Where He Can Do Good

Father Cooney and the 35th Indiana—part of the Union Army of the Ohio—spent their first year marching to and fro: from Kentucky and Tennessee (and back again) in the spring, summer and fall (by one account marching more than a thousand miles over the course of the year), sometimes seizing and guarding railroads. Father Cooney was not idle; like Father Corby, he engaged in a wide variety of activities to assist the men in temporal matters as well as spiritual ones. One of his most important duties involved collecting money from the soldiers on payday, becoming "a banker without fee or discount" and often handling tens of thousands of dollars at a time.[72]

For their part, the men of the 35th Indiana were glad to have Father Cooney with them. A correspondent visiting the regiment reported that "to say that he is much respected by the men of the regiment, is saying too little; he is loved by them" and added the following "rough and witty" anecdote as evidence of the feelings of the soldiers for their chaplain:

> *Around a blazing camp fire sat a few comrades smoking their "dudgheens" (short pipes) …Father Cooney came hurriedly along, evidently bent on a visit to some sick soldier. The little squad instantly rose to their feet with the hand to the cap. "Good evening, boys," said the Father, with one of his pleasant smiles, and hurried towards the hospital. "There he goes," said one of the group, "he's always where he can do good, and niver idle. The likes iv him, God bless him, is not to be found betwixt here and the giant's causeway." "Thrue for ye, Tim, by gorra; his match coud'nt be found iv ye thraveled from Dan to Barsheeba," said his comrade. "He'll be sayin his bades among the stars, whin many of his callin' will be huntin' a dhrop of wather in a very hot climate."[73]*

Fighting began in earnest for the 35th Indiana on the very last day of 1862. "I am safe after being through the most terrible battle of the war," Father Cooney began a letter to his brother, adding, "I have time now to write you but a few words…My time now is very precious attending to the dying wounded." The battle to which he referred—at Stones River, Tennessee—was fought from December 31, 1862, to January 2, 1863, and was a terrible engagement, indeed; of all the major battles of the war, Stones River was distinguished by having the highest percentage of casualties among the forces engaged on both sides.[74]

The 35th Indiana was involved all three days of the battle, including skirmishing on the first two days and severe fighting on the third, within just yards of the determined enemy. "We lost of our regiment, killed on the field twenty-eight and wounded sixty-seven many of whom are since dead," Father Cooney continued. "And nothing but God's protection could have saved me," he added, "as I was in the midst of it the whole time." This was no idle boast. Colonel B.F. Mullen, commanding the 35th Indiana, mentioned the brave priest in his official report:

> *To Father Cooney, our chaplain, too much praise cannot be given. Indifferent as to himself, he was deeply solicitous for the temporal and spiritual welfare of us all. On the field he was cool and indifferent to danger, and in the name of the regiment, I thank him for his kindness and laborious attention to the dead and dying.*[75]

It was only the first of several official mentions of bravery that Father Cooney would earn over the course of the war.

HIS LAST FULL MEASURE

While the 35th Indiana and Father Cooney fought on the Union left at Stones River, other Notre Dame student-soldiers were also on the battlefield, including Frank Baldwin, who was engaged nearby with the 44th Indiana Infantry. Baldwin, a native of Elkhart, Indiana, attended Notre Dame from 1860 to 1861. Perhaps inspired by classmate William F. Lynch, the seventeen-year-old Baldwin left home in the summer of 1861 with friend George M. Keeley and traveled to Illinois to join Colonel Mulligan's 23rd Illinois Infantry. While Lynch missed the early battles of the 23rd in Missouri, Baldwin did not and was taken prisoner when Mulligan surrendered his command at Lexington; Baldwin was paroled soon after.

Baldwin returned home to Elkhart, yet against his parents' wishes, "the martial fire still burned in him at the exclusion of everything else." One day in early 1862, Baldwin and his friends Norman H. Strong and Cullen W. Green heard that the 48th Indiana Infantry regiment was leaving nearby Goshen for the front. The boys—all still under eighteen—went to the schoolhouse, bid farewell to their classmates, hid behind an old blacksmith shop and then jumped on the train carrying the regiment.[76]

The train carried the soldiers, Baldwin and his two companion stowaways to Paducah, Kentucky, where the 48th Indiana met a fleet of transports carrying the Union army to Fort Donelson. Baldwin, Strong and Green went down to the river and boarded a boat, where they happily found themselves among Elkhart men of the 44th Indiana Infantry. The boys indicated their desire to enlist but a company commander, Captain Albert Heath, refused them on account of their age. He told the boys that they could see the fight at Donelson, after which he would send them back home. The boys protested and declared that "they had come to fight and were going to fight anyway." Heath consulted with his commander, Colonel Hugh B. Read, who agreed to let them join. Baldwin was with the 44th Indiana through all its engagements of 1862, including at Shiloh, where he was wounded.[77]

On December 31, 1862, Baldwin—since promoted to third sergeant—and the 44th Indiana were engaged in the first day of the Battle of Stones River. The regiment marched in line of battle through an open field, where it discovered the enemy making a flank movement on its right, in a wood bordering the field. The men made a stand at the edge of the wood in their front but were soon ordered to advance, with the line of the enemy soon coming into sight. They continued their advance, coming within a hundred yards of the enemy's line. The 44th Indiana opened fire; the Confederate line replied and advanced as well, and its flanking force opened a galling crossfire on the Hoosiers. The 44th Indiana held the position as long as it could and then fell back to its battery and re-formed its lines.

When the order was given to fall back, Baldwin and Green—himself recently promoted to lieutenant—were standing together behind a tree. They fell back into the open space and started with the rest of the regiment across the field, exposed to the crossfire. As they neared a fence, the two friends were running side by side. Green called out, "Throw your gun over the fence," pitching his own over and following it to the opposite side. Green pressed on but never saw Frank Baldwin alive again.[78]

A few days later, Green asked for permission to take a detail of six men to find his constant companion. Green found Baldwin just on the other side of the fence from where he had cried out to his friend. Baldwin had been struck by a musket ball—perhaps while climbing over the fence—which had entered under his right shoulder blade, passed through his heart and exited out the left side. The detail placed

Notre Dame student-soldier Frank Baldwin was killed in action at the Battle of Stones River. Detail from the Elkhart (Indiana) Soldiers and Sailors Monument. See the conclusion for more information on the monument. *Corrine Rypka.*

Baldwin's body in a crude coffin and buried it in the hospital yard. When, two months later, a family friend came to retrieve Baldwin's remains, Lieutenant Green accompanied him to the cemetery with a detail of soldiers, who exhumed the body and placed it in a metallic coffin. Baldwin was then laid to rest in the family's mausoleum in Grace Lawn Cemetery in Elkhart.

Thus Frank Baldwin joined Notre Dame's Michael Quinlan, John Lonergan, Fathers Lévêque and Bourget and Sisters Fidelis and Elise in giving their "last full measure of devotion" in the war, each in his or her own way. It had been a hard year for Notre Dame.

Chapter 5

FRIENDS IN DEED

Amicu certus in re incerta cernitur
(A sure friend is known when in difficulty)
—*Quintus Ennius, 300 BC*

As the architect of a Catholic institution in what was still missionary territory, Father Sorin needed patrons, and he found them in influential and charitable families near and far. As the principal shepherd to a growing family of students, he also found that he could extend his own favors when they were needed. One of those families, the Shermans, were the recipients of many favors involving Father Sorin and Notre Dame during the Civil War years.

William Tecumseh Sherman was born in Lancaster, Ohio, on February 8, 1820, the third son and sixth child (of eleven) of Charles Robert and Mary Hoyt Sherman. His father, a noted Ohio lawyer, was appointed a justice of the Ohio Supreme Court in 1823. While riding the judicial circuit, Charles suddenly fell ill and died. William's brother, John, recalled that their father had "left the family poor in everything but friends." Those friends came forward to help Mary Sherman raise her children. Neighbor Thomas Ewing asked for the "brightest of the lot" and promised to "make a man of him"; he took the nine-year-old William Sherman by the hand back to his home.[79]

As a United States senator, in 1836 Ewing secured an appointment to the United States Military Academy at West Point for his foster son. Sherman graduated from West Point in 1840 and married Ewing's daughter, Ellen, in 1850. Sherman resigned his commission in 1853 and took turns as a banker and lawyer before he assumed the position of superintendent at the fledgling Louisiana State Seminary of Learning (since Louisiana State University). He succeeded in getting the school on a firm foundation, but he resigned his position in January 1861 on the eve of Louisiana's secession from the Union.

Sherman rejoined the regular army in mid-1861, but his initial service was conducted in fits and starts: His brave leadership of a brigade of volunteers at the First Battle of Bull Run in July 1861 prompted President Abraham Lincoln to promoted him to brigadier general of volunteers, but in late 1861, he suffered from nervous exhaustion (although some uncharitably thought him insane) and was relieved from duty. He recovered in early 1862 and served in supporting roles until he was given command of a division under Ulysses S. Grant. His first great test was at the Battle of Shiloh in April 1862. He distinguished himself there and in campaigns and battles throughout the war. All the while, Ellen was his closest confidante, correspondent and advocate.

GOOD ROUGH PLAY

By the start of the war, the Shermans had six children: Maria Ewing ("Minnie"), Mary Elizabeth ("Lizzie"), William Tecumseh Jr. ("Willy"), Thomas Ewing ("Tommy"), Eleanor Mary and Rachel Ewing. As the fall of 1862 approached, Ellen Sherman gave thought to where she would send the older ones to school. "I think I will send Minnie and Willy up to Notre Dame. They *must* have religious instruction, so that they will have strong faith," she wrote her husband. In her eyes, the choice was ideal: her brother, Philemon Ewing, had a son, Tommy, at the school (and daughters at Notre Dame's sister-school, St. Mary's), and she was impressed with the campus, academics and, of course, the religious training.[80]

Ellen was confident that her husband would give his approval, but Minnie's heartfelt postscript in a June 1862 letter to her "Dearest Papa" ("Will you please let me go to school at Notre Dame") must have helped. For his part, the general wrote, "In your last you asked to answer about sending the children to Notre Dame. I think you had better keep them near you always, but you know best." In early October, Ellen took Willy to Indiana (Minnie had gone ahead with Philemon Ewing) and enrolled him in the "minim" (grammar school) department.[81]

Major General William T. Sherman and son Thomas Sherman (circa 1865). *University of Notre Dame Archives*.

Within days of their arrival, Ellen could already report that "Willy wants to stay. Tommy Ewing has had him out horseback-riding already and he feels quite important to be at college." Willy certainly took to "college" life with great zeal; over the course of the school year, Ellen wrote her husband, "Willy is happy and full of fun. He has more outdoor exercise and good rough play up there [at Notre Dame] than he would have at home." And in another letter: "I take it he has scuffled, kicked, and played enough, for he has worn out all his pants, and I am officially notified that 'Master W.T. Sherman needs two more pants' to scuffle, kick, and play in."[82]

Both Minnie and Willy wrote their parents from school. Just after New Year's Day in 1863, Willy wrote to his mother: "I hope you had a merry Christmas…we are all very well at the College and the Academy. We will all have a very nice time skatin when freezes over…I get to see Minnie very often…The boys are going to read addresses at the night of the Epephany and are all so going to have plays." In May, he wrote to his father: "We are going in swimming today or tomorrow…They had a play at St. Marys last night…and Minnie had a part in it. I send my best love to you."[83]

June 1863 brought the annual commencement exercises, and Ellen wrote to her husband with just pride:

The year at Notre Dame has been a great benefit to [Willy] in many respects. I was very proud of him at the Exhibition when I heard his name called for six premiums…Minnie did equally well in her studies & stood as high in classes as a girl of her age could have done… Neither she or Willy got the first honor in their circle but they received second honors in them & considering how very strict the rules are I could not blame them for not receiving the first…I was delighted with the Institutions the country & the charming situation. Minnie is anxious to return and Willy is willing to do so.[84]

A THRILLING LETTER TO NOTRE DAME

"Please write me soon if you have time," Willy begged his father in a letter. William T. Sherman did correspond with Willy and Minnie during the war, probably more often than one might expect given his important responsibilities. To Minnie, he wrote to inspire ("When you study, study hard…and when you are done with your books let your mind run free"); to tease ("Tell [your sister] Lizzie I know she will beat you in learning Books"); and to frankly convey the realities of war ("I ought not to make many promises for I daily see too many officers buried by the roadside, or carried to the rear maimed and mangled to count on much of a future").[85]

In a letter to Willy at Notre Dame, written shortly after the Battle of Shiloh in April 1862, Sherman thanked his young son for his "first rate" letter, enclosed a "spur from the Boot of a dead Rebel Captain," complained about the newspapermen ("[they] are afraid to be where the fighting is…afterward…they are very brave") and teased that "I want you…to study hard so that when you…are old enough you can let me & Mama rest." The general almost always closed with regards for Father Sorin, Mother Angela and the teachers, promising Minnie: "[T]ell your teachers that if I survive this war…I will not forget those who are kind and good to my Minnie and Willy."[86]

The general's letter written from his headquarters during the siege of Vicksburg, Mississippi, must have been thrilling reading for Willy and his schoolmates at Notre Dame:

> *I got your letter by* [Father] *Carrier…who came here from South Bend, and told me all about you and Minnie, Tommy Ewing and Elly. Of course I was very glad to hear from you by one who had come straight from you.*
>
> *Mama tells me that she will be at your examinations on the 28ᵗʰ and that as soon as it is over she will take you all home to Lancaster. Indeed would I like to meet you all there, but you are old enough now to know that I must be here with the Army, which is besieging the city of Vicksburg.*

"We have had many battles," he continued, "and we are working day and night to make many other [ditches] so that when we next attack, we expect to get inside Vicksburg, when we must have another great battle." He told Willy of his five horses and the ground around Vicksburg, which he described as "very broken, the hills steep, and hollows dark and filled with cane brake, the same kind of cane the boys use for fishing." Of the cane, he added news of a special gift:

> *It occurred to me you would like to have a fishing pole from the battlefield, so I had about a dozen cut and put up nicely…Give one to Tom Sherman, one to Tommy Ewing, and the rest distribute among*

your friends and tell them that they were gathered close up to Vicksburg, right on a battlefield on which thousands have already been killed, and thousands more will be.

Every cane has vibrated to the sound of near fifty thousand cannonballs fired with intent to kill, and it may be that more than one poor fellow has crawled to the shade of the leaves to die. Each one is therefore a precious memento. I felt you would prefer them to any book or toy bought with money.

"Of me you will always hear much that is bad, and much that is good," Sherman wrote in closing the letter to Willy. "The world is full of good and bad men and they have their reasons to praise or blame others. But you and my children will feel and know that I am always good to them, for they are growing up to fill stations higher and better than any I now fill and must be prepared," he added.[87]

THE CHAPLAIN AND THE BELEAGUERED CITY

That William T. Sherman referred to Father Carrier in his letter to Willy was fitting: it was Ellen Sherman who had asked Father Sorin to send one of his priests to her husband's army. Her brothers, General Hugh Boyle Ewing and Captain Charles Ewing (the general's foster brother and brother-in-law, respectively), were also in the army at Vicksburg. As devout as their sister, they had both expressed a wish to have a priest assigned to Grant's army, which was without a Catholic chaplain in all its ranks. Father Sorin sent Father Carrier immediately to oblige her fervent hope that the chaplain would "get down there in time to prepare many a poor soul for the last dread journey."[88]

The general had explained in his letter to Willy that a costly battle with the Confederates could be avoided if "their provisions will give out, for no person can get out or in Vicksburg without our consent, and if they have nothing to eat, they will starve or give up." Only days later, the Confederate army at Vicksburg did surrender, after a forty-seven-day siege. Father Carrier got a firsthand look at the conquered city the day after the surrender. He secured a souvenir—the last issue of the city's newspaper, printed on wallpaper—which he sent to Father Sorin as "a memento of a beleaguered but now fallen stronghold...[to] show all future generations to what extremities the Confederates were reduced."[89]

Of the city, Father Carrier wrote to Father Sorin that "there is not one single house in the whole city which has not been more or less damaged," adding that "[it] really saddens one to see so many ruins." He located the Catholic church in Vicksburg, which he happily reported "was but slightly injured." Indeed, one Vicksburg citizen remembered that while the "soaring light spire and gold cross" of the church was one of the most prominent features of the town, it was "never defaced by the fire of the enemy," though he was not sure "whether this was chance or intention." (Surely General Sherman did not have such "control" over cannonballs; it's equally sure that he would not risk the ire of his devout wife or his zealous but genial chaplain by purposely aiming at the church tower!) Father Carrier met Father Henzi, the weary but friendly assistant pastor—a fellow Frenchman—who "had lived for fifteen days in his cellar…for fear of the shells."[90]

Upon returning to camp, Father Carrier learned that the army was departing right away. "It really had been painful for me to pull down my tents and leave my nice cozy quarters! I had become strongly attached to the place," Father Carrier recalled. The days-long march in the hot and humid Mississippi clime was debilitating. Absent their wagons, "we had neither tent nor beds but we had the canopy of heaven…and the bare ground," Father Carrier wrote Father Sorin. Food was also scarce—"not a cracker to crack," he wrote—but Father Carrier took it all with good cheer. "Bah! This is for a follower of the Holy Cross a mere *bagatelle* [trifle]," he wrote Father Sorin, adding, "We…resumed our march, strictly fasting, although it was neither Lent, nor ember day, nor vigil." The Union army chased remnants of the Confederate army out of Vicksburg and then encamped on the Big Black River.[91]

A SOLDIER'S FATE

"I wish you could see [Vicksburg] for a minute, but it is not right for children to be here, as the danger is too great," William T. Sherman had written Willy, but after the surrender the general felt confident enough to invite his family to his new camp on the Big Black. Sherman assured his father-in-law that the camp was "one of the best possible," that it "combine[d] comfort, retirement, safety, and beauty" and that he had "no apprehensions on the score of health." Ellen was thrilled at the invitation, writing, "We are all so crazy to go…The thought of going down to you has spread sunshine over everything—all have gone to bed to dream happy dreams & my own heart is full of joy—God grant that nothing may occur to mar the happiness we anticipate."[92]

Ellen, daughters Lizzie and Minnie and sons Willy and Tommy—Ellie and Rachel, only toddlers, remained at home—arrived in mid-August, and their days were full from dawn to dusk. "The children are happy and well and their Father is delighted to have them with him," Ellen wrote her mother. "Minnie and Willy ride horseback with him while Lizzie and Tommy drive about with me in the carriage." Ellen also had the comfort of a Notre Dame chaplain, adding, "Sunday we attended Mass at Hugh's headquarters and heard Father Carrier preach."[93]

For Willy, especially, the visit was a great adventure, and he reveled being so close to his father, who recalled, "[He] took the most intense interest in the affairs of the army. He was a great favorite with the soldiers, and used to ride with me on horseback in the numerous drills and reviews…He was called a sergeant in the regular battalion, learned the manual of arms, and regularly attended the parade and guard-mounting of the Thirteenth [U.S. Infantry], back of my camp." In a letter a few weeks later, Sherman thanked the soldiers for the kindness they had extended to his son that summer, writing that "Willie was, or thought he was, a sergeant in the Thirteenth. I have seen his eyes brighten, his heart beat, as he beheld the battalion under arms, and asked me if they were not *real* soldiers."[94]

In late September, duty called again, and Sherman was asked to move his corps from its camp on the Big Black to Chattanooga, Tennessee. Sherman dispatched his troops immediately and followed quickly with his family, all boarding the steamer *Atlantic* bound for Memphis. Both Minnie and Willy became ill on the voyage. The usually energetic boy was listless and weary as they pushed up the river. A regimental surgeon on board the *Atlantic* examined the little soldier and declared him quite sick—perhaps fatally so—with "camp fever." As soon as the steamer reached Memphis on October 2, 1863, the Shermans took Willy to the Gayoso Hotel and called for the town's best physicians, yet the ministrations were to no avail.

Notre Dame's Father Carrier had traveled with the family and stayed at Willy's side almost constantly. Sensing the seriousness of Willy's condition, the chaplain began to gently speak to Willy of heaven. "He told me that he was willing to die if it was God's will," Father Carrier wrote Ellen a few weeks later, "but it pained him to leave his Father and Mother." He continued:

"Our Little Sergeant Willie" is buried in the Sherman family plot at Calvary Cemetery, St. Louis, Missouri. *Curtis Fears*.

He said this with an expression of such deep earnestness that I could hardly refrain from giving way to my feelings. I endeavored to soothe his sentiments of subdued regret. "Willy," I said quietly and calmly, "If God wishes to call you to Him now do not grieve, for He will carry you to Heaven and there you will meet your good Mother and Father again."
"Well," he breathed, with an air of singular resignation.[95]

Willy drifted in and out of sleep, waking only to inquire of the whereabouts of his prized rifle. "He never complained; how I wish he would have complained more!" Ellen wrote. Willy Sherman died the next day.[96]

You Can Always Count on a Notre Dame Boy

The family secured a metallic casket and held a military funeral, a battalion of the 13th U.S. Infantry acting as an escort from Memphis to Cairo, Illinois, to Lancaster, Ohio, where Willy was buried. "Of all my children he seemed the most precious," Sherman wrote in his memoirs, "and he seemed more than any of the children to take an interest in my special profession." Yet the war was still raging. "Being in the very midst of an important military enterprise, I had hardly time to pause and think of my personal loss," he added. Although both parents were most depressed at the loss, it was left to the prayerful Ellen to assuage the sorrow of Willy's brothers, sisters and grandparents over the coming year.[97]

In the summer of 1864, Ellen's mind again turned to the children's schooling. "[Minnie and Lizzie] are keen to go up to Notre Dame again," she wrote her husband, adding, "If I took them to Notre Dame I could also take Tommy…What do you say to it?" The general must have agreed, because in Ellen's next letter she declared, "The children are delighted by your permission to them to go to Notre Dame." Lizzie and Minnie were with the Holy Cross sisters at St. Mary's, and Tommy, like his late brother Willy, was now at Notre Dame as a minim. Unlike his brother, Tommy seemed to take more to his studies than to play, or was "more intensely school-boy," as Ellen put it. She wrote her husband that Tommy "has been ding-donging his story-books into my ears."[98]

Being the son of a famous father had its advantages as well as its challenges, and the young Tommy Sherman was no exception. The students, almost all of whom admired the general, liked to tease Tommy. "Your pa says he's going through Georgia like a whirlwind! Yeah, he says he's going to have Christmas dinner on the sea-coast! Can't be done, Tommy, it's crazy!" Indignantly, Tommy took pen in hand and complained to his father of the rank injustice of his fellow students. "As for me," he added, "you can count on ONE boy at Notre Dame that believes you can do it!"[99]

Just months later, with the war at an end and the country at peace, the Sherman family returned to Notre Dame, where the general had a chance to keep his promise to "not forget those who are kind and good to my Minnie and Willy."

Chapter 6
ABOVE AND BEYOND
THE CALL

A moment—'neath yon shelving stone—Within that awful field—
Those heroes bend in deep atone, While Death's dark shadows yield;
A soldier-priest, with hands extend Absolves their sins! Forgiven—
Short shrift was theirs, Faith makes amend Beneath approving heaven
—James J. Cresell, 1894

After the debacle at Fredericksburg in December 1862, Father Corby and the Irish Brigade returned to the camps they had occupied before the battle. Except for the short and ill-fated "Mud March" of Union general Ambrose Burnside, there would be no more fighting until spring, and Father Corby returned to his daily routine of ministering to the soldiers in camp and the sick in the hospital. In spite of, or because of, their losses at Fredericksburg, the men of the brigade were determined to make St. Patrick's Day (always a special day for the Irish) one to remember. Father Corby recalled with great pleasure the grandeur of the morning's religious ceremony, the fun of the day's sport and the bounty of the evening's dinner.

In late April 1863, the army was in motion and in early May engaged the Confederate army at Chancellorsville, Virginia, not far from the old battlefield at Fredericksburg. During the battle, Father Corby assisted the surgeons with the brigade's wounded at the Chancellor House. The mansion was also the Union army headquarters, and as such "the Confederates got exact range…and in a short time the location became 'very hot,'" Father Corby remembered. The Irish Brigade performed bravely, yet "the battle went against us," he wrote, and the army returned to its camps again.[100]

Two months later, the very weekend that Notre Dame's Father Carrier witnessed General Sherman's victorious conquest of Vicksburg, Father Corby was a thousand miles away and involved in the one of the most important battles of the Civil War; his seemingly small part in the drama would prove to be most memorable.

A HAND RAISED AT GETTYSBURG

About a month after the Battle of Chancellorsville, the Irish Brigade and the Army of the Potomac were once again on the march. They left their camps on the Rappahannock for a month-long trek of almost three hundred miles through Maryland and into Pennsylvania, where they met the Confederate army in the epic Battle of Gettysburg. On July 1, 1863, the Irish Brigade was almost fifteen miles away from Gettysburg, in Taneytown, Maryland. Upon hearing that the battle had started, the troopers resumed their march, and on July 2, the brigade was posted at Cemetery Ridge.

Late in the afternoon, just as the Irish Brigade was about to be ordered into the fray, Father Corby—realizing that he had no time to hear individual confessions—asked for an opportunity to give a general absolution to the soldiers in his charge. An officer in the brigade recalled the scene:

> *Father Corby stood upon a large rock in front of the brigade. Addressing the men, he explained what he was about to do, saying that each one could receive the benefit of the absolution by making a sincere act of contrition and firmly resolving to embrace the first opportunity of confessing their sins, urging them to do their duty well, and reminding them of the high and sacred nature of their trust as soldiers and the noble object for which they fought, ending by saying that the Catholic Church refuses Christian burial to the soldier who turns his back upon the foe or deserts his flag. The brigade was standing at "order arms," and as he closed his address, every man fell on his knees with head bowed down. Then, stretching his right hand toward the brigade, Father Corby pronounced the* [Latin] *words of the general absolution,* Dominus noster Jesus Christus vos absolvat… *The scene was more than impressive, it was*

awe-inspiring…I do not think there was a man in the brigade who did not offer up a heartfelt prayer. For some it was their last.[101]

The rite of general absolution had a centuries-long and storied tradition in the armies of Europe, but the officer's claim that "it was perhaps the first time it was ever witnessed on this continent" was an exaggeration. It had been performed by other priests—even by Father Corby himself—before other battles during the Civil War. Still, the sheer number of men and the surroundings made the sight all the more impressive and memorable. "My eye covered thousands of officers and men," Father Corby recalled years later. "The situation really reminded one of the day of judgment…so great were the whirlwinds of war then in motion."[102]

The situation also mesmerized officers near the scene who were not part of the Irish Brigade. "Even Maj. Gen. Hancock removed his hat and…bowed in reverential devotion," Father Corby recalled. General Samuel K. Zook, commanding another brigade in the same division as the Irish Brigade, witnessed the scene and exclaimed to an aide: "My God! That was the most impressive sight I have ever heard of." Father Corby recalled that a captain rode up to him a week after the battle and stated: "While I have often witnessed ministers make prayers I never witnessed one so powerful as the one you made that day."[103]

Father Corby took satisfaction that inspiring scenes like his at Gettysburg—but mostly his daily work among the soldiers—removed a great amount of anti-Catholic prejudice in the ranks, just as the sisters' work in the hospital did. "When men stand in common danger, a fraternal feeling springs up between them and generates a…charitable sentiment that often leads to most excellent results," he concluded.[104]

A Gallant Act

Long after the Civil War was over, St. Clair Augustine Mulholland—onetime commander of the Irish Brigade's 116th Pennsylvania Infantry—made a special effort to honor and promote the veterans of the brigade. He was a fervent friend and admirer of Father Corby, and in 1893 he spearheaded an effort to obtain the Medal of Honor for Father Corby in recognition of his courage under fire during the war. Mulholland specifically asked that it be given for Corby's "very gallant and most remarkable act in preaching a most patriotic sermon and administering the religious rite of General absolution on the battlefield at Gettysburg."[105]

In his recommendation to the War Department, Mulholland referred to Father Corby as a "Fighting Chaplain" for whom "no spot was too dangerous or too much exposed to the fire of the enemy." W.L. O'Grady, an officer in the 88th New York, added that Father Corby was "a man whose courage was not surpassed by the bravest soldier of our armies, whose unflinching devotion on the march, in camp and under fire made him eminent, whose magnificent conduct at Gettysburg has become historical, one of the most picturesque and beautiful incidents of that great drama."[106]

Unfortunately, the War Department turned down the application. "The action of Father Corby was undoubtedly meritorious and highly commendable and his name will go down to history embalmed with the affection of comrades and patriots," a War Department bureaucrat wrote Mulholland, but "the case does not, however, come within the law authorizing the issue of medals."[107]

The official's closing declaration, "The memory of his noble deeds will be more enduring than a bronze medal," while true, did not assuage the disappointment of Mulholland and O'Grady. Indeed, Mulholland seemed to take the failure quite personally. "The [refusal] ends all our hopes and aspiration," Mulholland wrote Father Corby, adding that "I have done my best and only regret that I did not succeed." Not surprisingly, the effort's failure did not reduce the importance of Father Corby in the eyes of the brigade veterans. "I do not look on [the refusal] so gloomily as Genl. Mulholland," James Quinlan of the Irish Brigade Association wrote to Father Corby. He told Father Corby that at the veterans' summer meeting "the boys were most enthusiastic in your behalf and the resolutions [in your honor] were passed with a 'whoop.'"[108]

For his part, Father Corby also regretted not being rewarded the Medal of Honor. While this was a seemingly uncharacteristic sentiment for the selfless priest, his chief biographer explained that Father Corby was not disappointed on his own account but rather was "motivated by a desire to remind Americans of the patriotic service that thousands of Catholics had rendered in the late war." In fact, the War Department official's confidence that Father Corby's deed at Gettysburg would endure was prescient. Many who witnessed it would never forget the scene; it has been immortalized on canvas, in poetry, in literature and in modern film. Most importantly, it forever attached the University of Notre Dame—through Father Corby—to one of the war's most pivotal battles:

Old Gettysburg yet lives to tell When night each star bends down
How rebel hail of shot and shell, Plow'd thro' that loyal town
An well hath Gettysburg relied On soldier boys' brave deed
While Little Round Top points with pride To Corby's loyal creed[109]

A PATRIOTIC HEART

Although Father Corby did not earn a Medal of Honor, he and the university would be able to take pride in the fact that a Notre Dame student-soldier did earn the medal in recognition of his valor under fire

Orville T. Chamberlain.
Indiana Historical Society.

on another battlefield in the summer of 1863, hundreds of miles from Gettysburg. That brave young man was Orville T. Chamberlain.

Chamberlain was born in 1841 in Leesburgh, Indiana. His family moved to Elkhart, Indiana, when he was but two years old. In his teens, Chamberlain clerked in his father's drugstore, learned the printer's trade and taught school at a local schoolhouse. He entered the University of Notre Dame in 1860 and after a year of study was awarded the degree "Master of Accounts." He returned the next year to take advanced classes in English and the classics and returned home to Elkhart in June 1862. A few weeks later—"yielding to the prompting of his patriotic heart"—he enlisted as a private in the 74th Indiana Infantry.[110]

Chamberlain's service and thoughts are preserved in a collection of more than eighty wartime letters that he wrote to home and friends, now held by the Indiana Historical Society. The letters begin with his enlistment at Fort Wayne and his initial encampment in Indianapolis in August 1862. He happily reported that "I saw quite a number of my [Notre Dame] acquaintances there," and he wrote regularly of classmates in his own regiment. The regiment moved to Bowling Green, Kentucky, in September 1862; Chamberlain became quite ill but was nursed back to health by a comrade in a private home and wrote home on "captured" official stationery left by retreating Rebels.[111]

Over the course of a year in the Union army, Orville Chamberlain was promoted from private to sergeant and then to lieutenant; by the next summer, he was in command of Company G of the 74th Indiana. After a year of drilling, marching, countermarching and guard duty, the war finally started in earnest for Chamberlain and his men.

A PERILOUS JOURNEY

In mid-August 1863, the regiment—then occupying middle Tennessee— moved south as Major General William Rosecrans consolidated his scattered forces and successfully forced the Rebel army out of Chattanooga. Confederate general Braxton Bragg was determined to reoccupy the city and launched an attack on the Union army in mid-September. Late on September 18, 1863, the 74th Indiana struck out on an all-night march on the Chattanooga Road and arrived at Chickamauga early the next morning. The official report declared that the regiment halted and took a hasty cup of coffee—"'hasty' indeed it was, for the few who got any," Chamberlain recalled.[112]

On September 19, the regiment was placed in line of battle. During the fighting in the morning and the afternoon, the men of the 74th Indiana had discarded their knapsacks and blankets. "We never saw them again," Chamberlain remembered, and when they bivouacked that night they had no food or water, little to make themselves comfortable and were also under orders not to start fires. "Some succeeded in getting some straw. More had to sleep on the bare ground," Chamberlain wrote, adding that "[i]t was very cold...All were worn out by the terrible experiences of the day. It was a terrible, cheerless, cold, desolate, miserable night."[113]

The next day, Chamberlain recalled, "We were lying behind our hastily built breastworks, lying as flat upon the earth as we could flatten ourselves, to avoid the fire from the enemy's musketry which was turned upon us...Every movement, or exposure invited and received a storm of bullets from the vastly superior force of the enemy in front," Chamberlain recalled. At this point, the regiment was sorely in need of more ammunition, and Chamberlain informed Lieutenant Colonel Baker that the 9th Indiana Infantry had a large supply of ammunition. "He knew I was well acquainted with Company C of that regiment and asked me if I would undertake personally to go that Regiment and beg what ammunition I could and bring it back, if possible, to our Regiment. I told him I would make the effort, which I did successfully."[114]

Successful, indeed: Orville T. Chamberlain earned the Medal of Honor for the feat (though it took more than thirty years to secure the award). His own words and even the official citation ("While exposed to a galling fire, went in search of another regiment, found its location, procured ammunition from the men thereof, and returned with the ammunition to his own company") belie the danger involved. A more fitting description of the episode appeared in a family history many years later:

> *On the field of Chickamauga, the Seventy-fourth and Tenth Indiana had been lying in the outer trenches under constant fire. Five lines of Confederate Infantry were lined up against one in the trenches and the Unionists were not only outnumbered but out of ammunition. Every time one of their number raised his head, a sharpshooter sent a bullet after it. Ammunition was wanted and knowing that the Ninth Indiana, a mile and a quarter away on the firing line, had plenty, Lieutenant Chamberlain gathered all the haversacks he could secure and started on his perilous journey. The moment he rose to his feet and started,*

there was a fusillade of bullets fired at him as he passed down the line; but he still kept on, running low on the ground, dodging from stump to stump and boulder to boulder, crawling over open spaces like a snake and bounding like a rabbit, he finally reached the trenches of the Ninth; loaded his pockets and haversacks; arranged for a wagon-load of ammunition to follow as quickly as possible, and was off again through the rain of leaden bullets, which followed his course back to his regiment where he delivered the ammunition to his commanding officer. While he received several slight wounds, his hat was shot away and his clothing riddled, he escaped serious injury.[115]

Nearly a month after the battle, Orville finally had a chance to pen a short letter home. Despite the brutal autumn fighting in Georgia and Tennessee, he assured his family by writing: "I am still alive, and that's saying enough to be thankful for."[116]

The same sentiment could be said for all of the Notre Dame men and women serving in the war at the end of that pivotal year.

Chapter 7

CAMPUS ROWS

In times of war, and especially of national or civil war, all the passions of the poor human heart are to be dreaded.

—Father Edward Sorin

The Civil War had significant effects on colleges and universities across the country: declining enrollments due to student and faculty enlistments in the Union and Confederate armies; fiscal problems brought on by declining enrollment and exacerbated by wartime inflation; concerted enemy movements in or around campuses; and inflamed partisan and sectional passions among the students. At the least, these challenges could disrupt the order of campus life; at worst, they could result in the institution closing its doors.

Each university addressed these challenges in its own way. Some survived by boosting enrollments of younger students in their companion preparatory schools. Others, like Oberlin, admitted women for the first time. Among the more interesting strategies—in anticipation of veteran benefits of the twentieth century—was to attract student-soldiers to return and finish their interrupted studies; some colleges even offered free tuition. Rampant wartime inflation put a squeeze on faculty salaries, but increasing pay was simply not practical for some colleges with already strained budgets. Obviously, universities in the Confederate states were particularly prone to occupation, and sometimes physical destruction, of their buildings and grounds, but even schools in the North—Gettysburg College being a famous example—saw their campuses turned into battlegrounds and hospitals.

Student unrest on American college campuses—while more famous and familiar in Vietnam-era protests—can actually be traced as far back as the American Revolution. Likewise, students in the Civil War era demonstrated their feelings and opinions—pro-Union, anti-administration or (very suspicious to some) apparent indifference—through patriotic meetings, mock funerals, commencement exercises, student literary magazines, visiting speakers and other events and outlets. Not surprisingly, some of these turned quite violent.[117]

While Father Sorin could justly boast in 1861 that "the hard times this year, which caused half the colleges of the country to close, [have] thus far had no such effect on this institution," he did still face many of these same wartime challenges. For example, while he declared that "[t]he number of boarders has even exceeded that of last year," he also admitted that "[t]hese same hard times have compelled everyone to look more carefully to a stricter economy." Yet, in the end, the optimistic superior could conclude that "if there has been suffering in one sense, there has been gain in another; the morale of the institute has been the gainer, and that is the main point."[118]

A Melting Pot

Father Sorin directly attributed the increase in the number of students to Notre Dame's "distance from the theater of war," which was good enough reason for parents in the Confederate states to send their sons to Notre Dame during the conflict. For example, wartime student James M. McCormack recalled that "opportunities for education in the South were at a low ebb" during the war and that "at least thirty new boys were listed from that section." That number included James himself, the first of three McCormack boys from Nashville, Tennessee, to attend Notre Dame over the next decade. He also counted among the wartime Nashville matriculates five boys from the Burns family, two boys named Pilcher and Tom Flanigan, whom he remembered as "the leading baseball player."[119]

James McCormack was quite right about the influx of Southern students during the war but may have actually underestimated the number. A survey of enrollment records that included all types of students—minims in the grammar school program, young men enrolled in the university and boys attached to the "Manual Labor" school—

reveals a significant increase in students from the Confederate states over the course of the war years. Fewer than five students were enrolled each year from 1860 to 1862, and they from only two states (Louisiana and Virginia), but that number had increased to thirteen for the school year of 1862–63. By the end of the war, more than forty students—from Tennessee (especially), Louisiana, Arkansas and Mississippi—called Notre Dame home. The "border states," especially Kentucky and Missouri, contributed more students still (see Table I).[120]

While one can take the boy out of the South, it is an entirely different matter to take the South out of the boy, and given the mix of sectional sensibilities, the "melting pot" at Notre Dame did boil over from time to time.

TABLE I. WARTIME ENROLLMENT AT UNIVERSITY OF NOTRE DAME

	1860–61	1861–62	1862–63	1863–64	1864–65	1865–66	Total	%
Midwest								78.6
Indiana	73	74	78	113	130	159	627	27.2
Illinois	59	47	67	113	140	181	607	26.3
Michigan	25	27	36	44	41	70	243	10.5
Ohio	17	26	37	45	50	64	239	10.4
Iowa	3	5	3	5	10	18	44	1.9
Wisconsin	1	3	2	6	19	13	44	1.9
Kansas	1				2	2	5	0.2
Minnesota						2	2	0.1
Far West								1.0
New Mexico					5	6	11	0.5
California	2	3	2	1	1	1	10	0.4
Colorado					1	1	2	0.1

	1860–61	1861–62	1862–63	1863–64	1864–65	1865–66	Total	%
Northeast/New England								7.1
Pennsylvania	7	15	13	11	15	24	85	3.7
New York	2	4	8	11	21	16	62	2.7
Massachusetts	2	1	2	1		1	7	0.3
New Jersey				1	2	2	5	0.2
Washington, D.C.			1	2	2		5	0.2
Border States								6.7
Kentucky			3	19	45	36	103	4.5
Missouri	1	2	2	6	13	16	40	1.7
Maryland	3	4	4	1			12	0.5
Confederate States								5.7
Tennessee			8	18	32	37	85	3.7
Louisiana	4	3	5	5	6		23	1.0
Mississippi			1	5	3		9	0.4
Arkansas					3		3	0.1
Virginia	1						1	<0.1
Foreign								0.9
Canada	1	3	1	1	2	4	12	0.5
France		2	1				3	0.1
Cuba	1	1	1				3	0.1
Ireland				1			1	<0.1
England					1			<0.1

STUDENT LIFE

Historians can thank James McCormack for leaving one of the best descriptions of student life at Notre Dame during the war years. "My first semester at Notre Dame all furnishings were very simple, really crude," he recalled, adding that "the real improvements took place during the second semester. Steam heat superseded wood fires, as no coal was used in that section. All the rooms and halls had individual stoves and it took the time of one Brother to keep the fires alive."[121]

Indeed, Father Sorin wrote that directly because of the war, "laborers became so scarce that it was hard to find men to cut fire wood" and that the school's council found itself "face to face with the almost impossible task of obtaining the amount of wood necessary for the winter, which had already set in." After the "most serious deliberation," the council resolved to introduce steam heating (as had already been done at St. Mary's). It was already November, and "there was not a day to spare," Father Sorin continued, adding that "the work was urged forward with all possible haste, and by Christmas the college was heated satisfactorily and economically."[122]

James McCormack also remembered improvements in the sleeping arrangements:

> *Cotton mattresses were introduced to take the place of ticking stuffed with straw or corn shucks. From then on the boys snored louder and longer. The students seemed happier, as they felt Notre Dame was considering their comfort as well as their education. Better living conditions brought about an increase of students each year during my time at Notre Dame so that beds had to be put in the galleries of Washington Hall to take care of the overflow.*[123]

As a new soldier, Orville T. Chamberlain recalled the crowded conditions during his school days, writing in late August 1862 that his unit had "marched through [Louisville] to a house where we stayed overnight. A thousand men in one room is worse than the dormitories at Notre Dame."[124]

Of a typical day as a student, McCormack recalled:

> *Wednesday was the recreation day instead of Saturday. Life started every morning at half past five during my four years, but since then I have forgotten all about the rising sun. We went to Mass on*

Wednesday mornings—that was the only required church attendance during the week. The real work of the day started with a study hour at six o'clock, breakfast at seven, dinner at twelve and supper at six p.m. We returned to the study hall at seven and at eight we retired after a very short day that began at five thirty a.m. So far as living was concerned, the boys never had reason to complain. The food was plain, but bountifully served. We had the usual supply of turkey and mince pie on holidays—in fact, I can still taste the delicious pies and bread made by the good Sisters of the Holy Cross.[125]

Orville Chamberlain agreed with McCormack on the quality of the table fare, writing home before the war: "Our diet here is not luxurious, unless you think 'luxurious' to be derived from the Latin *lux* and make it partake of its original signification ["light"]; still we are in no danger of starvation, and they get up pretty good dinners." Of church attendance, Orville grumbled that "[w]e have to attend…a great deal here" but admitted that the previous week's sermon had "suited me exactly."[126]

McCormack might be forgiven for his dubious recollection that "the boys never saw South Bend except on arriving and departing from Notre Dame." To be sure, Father Sorin did everything possible to keep his students from town; if they had to go for a purchase or other business, they were required to be in the company of a prefect. Still, unauthorized forays did happen, especially to imbibe at South Bend taverns. One school history notes: "There is hardly a page of the disciplinary record on which it is not written…'this student, arrested for intoxication and lodged in the South Bend jail, was sent home.'" Father Sorin placed notices in the local papers asking the citizens to report any serious misbehavior.[127]

FISTICUFFS

While Father Sorin was able to avoid the wartime "town versus gown" riots that plagued some schools, his own campus did witness some unrest. With enrollment increasing each year, including the influx of Southern students, Father Sorin recognized how "much more serious…the danger" of the dreaded "passions of the poor human heart" had become. Indeed, Father Sorin admitted to his superiors that, among the student body, "there was far from anything like unity of views…in political matters: the two camps were, on the contrary, clearly divided." He credited the school's heavenly patron for the fact that the young men at Notre Dame "lived in harmony even whilst their fathers and brothers were slashing one another some hundreds of miles away."[128]

Despite Father Sorin's representations, however, there were in fact some unpleasant incidents, as heated sectional arguments began in the classroom and on the playground. In one instance, John Walker—a "stout, handsome youth, aggressive and foremost in expressing his loathing for Southerners"—had a bitter dispute with another boy, who reciprocated with a kick to John's head. The school authorities, hearing of the row, decided to expel Walker's foe. A body of students protested the decision—some even refused to go to study hall in protest—but discipline finally prevailed.[129]

Even the Sherman family couldn't avoid fisticuffs. Minnie Sherman, who like her brother Willy had spent the summer of 1863 in her father's camp in Mississippi, had been constantly doted on by the soldiers and was somewhat spoiled upon her return to St. Mary's. Indeed, one sister recalled that the attention "seemed to have turned [Minnie's] head…for she seemed to think on her return that as her father ruled the army, she should rule the school."[130]

A celebration was planned for Washington's Birthday (always a special day at Notre Dame and St. Mary's) in 1864, but the sisters had forbidden the wearing of any partisan colors. Minnie, however, had pinned a small flag to her dress and, so decorated, met a Southern girl in the hall. The Southerner snatched the flag from Minnie's dress and stomped on it. Nothing happened for an hour, but then:

> *A carriage drove up at furious speed. Hardly waiting for the horses to stop, Mrs. Sherman jumped out, rushed into the recreation room, pinned a fresh [flag] on Minnie, and wanted to know why her daughter could not wear the flag her father offered his life for.*[131]

Mrs. Sherman's act emboldened Minnie's classmates; more Northern girls brought out their own colors and small decorations and prepared a larger flag for the night's festivities. The Southern girls took exception, and as one of the sisters recalled, "Words soon led to blows, and almost in an instant the whole school with few exceptions were engaged in a pitched battle."[132]

Of the incident, a wartime student at St. Mary's remembered:

The girls divided into two parts with flashing eyes and burning cheeks meant business and the Sister in charge…stood pale with the bell in her hand but no one paid any attention…hair was being torn out in handfuls faces were scratched and bleeding and it only seemed to be growing more desperate when "Young ladies!" in Mother Angela's voice brought them to their senses and she at once asked for an explanation… She told them to bring all flags and rosettes to her which was done, but the southern girls said the flag that caused the trouble had not been given up. Being refused again…the northerners were kept in. They…gave the flag to Katie Putnam…[S]he got out of the window, slid down the porch, ran over to the ladies' house and gave the flag to Mrs. Sherman who was there. She took it with a smile and handed it to Tommy, then a little boy, telling him to "guard the flag." He took it with an air of reverence, but Katie has it now, she says it is a poor homemade affair but quite a relic. [133]

It seems that the tensions did not end with the surrender at Appomattox in 1865. Late in 1866, the following notice of a vicious campus fight appeared in the *St. Joseph Valley Register*:

An affray occurred between two students named Parker and Donovan… Donovan is from Vicksburg, Mississippi, and, like many other students at Notre Dame from the Rebel States, entertains and expresses views not in harmony with the Union sentiments at the North, or with those held by Parker, who resides in Lafayette, in this State.

Out of this political difference, a previous quarrel had arisen between these two and very unfriendly feelings had continued to exist. Thanksgiving Day was a holiday for the students, and in the sports of the afternoon Parker and Donovan simultaneously approached the swing, each in a bad humor, trying to take possession and neither willing to give up to the other. Finally, they were induced to yield the swing to a third party, and retired. Threats passed between them, and Donovan picked up a club and threw it at Parker, but not hitting him. Parker picked up the same club and struck Donovan with it twice, first on his shoulder, then on his head, fracturing his skull.

The officers of the University took Parker in charge and protected him from the violence threatened by Donovan's rebel friends. The next morning, Parker was expelled from the University and sent home. Parker's father came back with him and tried to get the boy reinstated, but learning that the affray was more serious than supposed, he took him back home again without wasting much time in seeking to secure the object of his visit.

Donovan still lies in a critical condition, but it is thought he will recover. No legal steps have yet been taken in regard to the affray. [134]

Father Sorin took exception to the *Register*'s portrayal of the fracas, and a week later it published his letter in which he declared "that the little 'difference' alluded to did not originate in politics":

The students of thus Institution were never allowed to discuss political topics. Literary pursuits…could scarcely prove ought else but a failure, if either the study hall or the recreation ground were to be made an arena for such debates and strifes. During the war, one of our chief objects was to keep from their midst all discussions which might have entailed quarrels or dissensions; and now when peace is happily restored, one of our first aims is to cultivate among them the most friendly sentiments, entirely regardless of parties, which indeed we mostly ignore and wish to ignore.

And besides, Father Sorin added, "you will be pleased to hear that the young gentleman mentioned in your last issue as 'in a critical state,' is now around and nearly well." [135]

Chapter 8

VOTE EARLY AND OFTEN

If one looks closely, one will appreciate that there are as decisive moments in the life of institutions as in the life of armies. A bold initiative sometimes disconcerts a powerful enemy and brings about success otherwise unattainable.

—Father Edward Sorin

Elections in the States are generally an occasion of some commotion," Father Sorin wrote in 1864, adding that "[t]his year, amidst the horrors of war, they could not but be the object of general interest, seeing that on them depended the continuation or the termination of those same horrors." Seven hundred miles away, in the Union army lines surrounding Atlanta, Father Sorin's former student, Orville Chamberlain, expressed his own anxiety about the elections in a letter to his father: "Are we going home to vote? We all want to," he wrote, adding that "I especially want to…I want to vote for Old Abe."[136]

Father Sorin could hardly underestimate the "commotion" or the "general interest" surrounding the 1864 elections, which were certainly among the most important in the country's history. While the Confederate states did not participate in that year's canvass, the glow of the victories at Gettysburg and Vicksburg in 1863 had softened due to heavy Union losses in Virginia in the spring of 1864, and President Abraham Lincoln faced challenges from several quarters: Southern sympathizers in the Border States, Peace Democrats and even a threat from Radical Republicans. Still, he managed to secure his party's nomination.

One of the significant points of contention in that year's election was an unpopular draft. Congress had passed the first national conscription law in 1863, but the better part of each state's quotas—including Indiana's—was actually met through volunteers, many of whom were enticed by liberal bounties offered by local governments. Provisions in the law allowed men with the means to avoid the draft by paying a commutation fee or finding (and paying) a substitute, which prompted cries of "a rich man's war and a poor man's fight" and violent riots in some cities. The heavy losses in the spring campaign, though, required Lincoln to call for an additional 500,000 troops in July 1864, and antigovernment sentiment swelled again in advance of the elections.

In October 1864, Indiana was holding an election to fill the governor's seat and openings in the state legislature and the state's delegation to the House of Representatives. President Lincoln recognized the significance of the Hoosier State elections, writing to General William T. Sherman that "the loss of [Indiana], to the friends of the Government would go far toward losing the whole Union cause in maintaining the status quo." He added:

> *The draft proceeds, notwithstanding its strong tendency to lose us the State. Indiana is the only important State…whose soldiers cannot vote in the field. Any thing you can safely do to let her soldiers, or any part of them, go home and vote at the State election, will be greatly in point… This is, in no sense, an order, but is merely intended to impress you with the importance, to the army itself, of your doing all you safely can, yourself being the judge of what you can safely do.*[137]

Sherman at first protested, declaring, "Of course it is impossible…to send away a single man would be an injustice to the remainder," but in the end he allowed thousands of Indiana soldiers to go home (but not Orville Chamberlain or his comrades in the 74th Indiana). Like General Sherman, Father Sorin found that his own community at Notre Dame was not immune to the pressures of conscription or elections; in fact, for Notre Dame it became a sticky combination. Fortunately, Father Sorin's own bold strokes—his "stock-in-trade," a biographer declared—and those of powerful friends would keep the good father and the Notre Dame community out of the morass.[138]

FULL OF FIGHT?

"The new conscription law passed in the Senate yesterday," Father Sorin wrote in early 1863, concluding with some anxiety: "This time, unless there is miraculous intervention, the existence of the Community will be seriously under threat." Indeed, that summer, Father Sorin reported to his superior that "[b]y the beginning of June, the conscription law having been everywhere promulgated, all the Fathers and Brothers between the ages of eighteen and forty-five and of sound mind and body were registered for military service. Lots were to be drawn shortly, and this circumstance caused more than a little alarm across the Province."[139]

Conscription had some unique implications for Father Sorin's community: the provision to avoid the draft by procuring a substitute and exemptions for clergy and conscientious objectors. Indiana had set its commutation fee at a seemingly modest $200—other states had fees as high as $300—and substitutes could run from a few hundred to thousands of dollars; either course would have drained Father Sorin's already strained treasury as the brothers had no property or money of their own, having taken a vow of poverty.

As ordained clergy, the Holy Cross priests were exempt from the draft—though no fewer than seven of Notre Dame's priests had volunteered—but the Holy Cross brothers were not. Even the prospect of applying as conscientious objectors was not certain; one provost marshal refused to exempt a Catholic priest under the pretext that Catholics were historically a pugnacious lot. Father Sorin's superiors even suggested that he should transfer the brothers to a Holy Cross community in Canada.

Father Sorin had a different plan: he directed Father Carrier, still in the Union lines at Vicksburg, to write a letter to President Lincoln asking for the favor of being exempted from the service:

NOTRE DAME, IND.
September 28, 1863.
His Excellency ABRAHAM LINCOLN, President of the United States

SIR: The order of the Holy Cross, consisting of priests, brothers, and sisters, and whose principal house in the United States is situated at Notre Dame, State of Indiana, humbly appeals to your justice and goodness for a kind hearing.

We most respectfully venture to ask of Your Excellency the privilege of being exempted from the military service, or rather from bearing arms. Not, indeed, because we are opposed to the measures which our rightful Government thinks proper to adopt and enact for the vigorous prosecution of the war, for that is, we sincerely believe, the speediest way to effectually crush down rebellion and restore peace to the nation, but on account of our true devotion to the Union and the constant support we have willingly and cheerfully given to the Government in sending with our armies six priests as chaplains (one died in a hospital a victim of his devotion to his country's cause, and three others went at the expense of the order), and in our army and navy hospitals nearly forty sisters as nurses. To serve as chaplains or nurses we always willingly do, as it is in conformity with our vocation; but to bear arms even in a war we deem right and just is very repugnant to our religious and sacred calling; nay more, priests or clerics cannot shed blood without incurring ipso facto the censures of the church.

It is true that we may be dispensed from bearing arms in procuring substitutes, but we respectfully represent to Your Excellency that individuals in religious orders do not possess anything, and our house cannot possibly procure substitutes for all the priests, clerics, and brothers that will soon be drafted without exposing our establishments in the United States to inevitable ruin.

In consideration of these facts, we are fully confident that Your Excellency will grant our petition, and in so doing acquire our lively and eternal gratitude.

With great respect, we are, most respectfully, sir, your humble and obedient servants.

E. Sorin, C.S.C. Prov.
J.C. Carrier, C.S.C.[140]

Father Carrier obtained the endorsements of two influential men: Generals Sherman and Grant. Sherman's was rather simple: "I concur, but do not commit myself as to the legal questions involved," while Grant's was (uncharacteristically) wordy:

I would respectfully represent that the order herein applying for exemption have contributed largely of their services to the support of the war, and if any class is to be exempt from the present or any future draft, they have fully entitled themselves to such benefit. Respectfully referred for the consideration of the President, hoping that, if not inconsistent with law or the policy of the Government, that the favor asked will be granted.[141]

Arriving in Washington with the letter, Father Carrier had an interview with Secretary of War Stanton—and with President Lincoln—and the request for an exemption was granted. Yet all was not settled.

THE SUPERIOR AND THE SPEAKER

While Father Sorin may have eschewed partisan discussion among the student body at Notre Dame, he was politically astute himself. Thomas Low Nichols, in his book *Forty Years of American Life*, wrote of his firsthand impression of Father Sorin's political mind:

[He] *conversed like a thorough man of the world on education, politics, and society. It was evident that he read the newspapers as well as his breviary, and that he had a sharp eye to business, as well as to the propagation of the faith. He even told me, with a curiously quiet consciousness of power in his tone and manner, how he had put down some bigotry in the neighbourhood, which had at one time threatened them, by exercising the political influence given him by the votes of his community. "It is not necessary for us to vote," said he; "we have not that trouble; but the fact that we can do so whenever we choose, and defeat either party, is quite enough to make both treat us with a respectful consideration."*[142]

Father Sorin's "quiet consciousness of power" was put to the test in a match with an equally astute politician: Schuyler Colfax of nearby South Bend, Indiana. A native of New York, Colfax had moved to northwest Indiana as a teenager with his mother and stepfather. Even as a young man, Colfax was politically aware—he held a (minor) county office at the age of fifteen—and he frequently wrote articles on state affairs for local newspapers and even publications as far removed from Indiana as Horace Greeley's *New York Tribune*. At nineteen, Colfax became editor of the local pro-Whig *South Bend Free Press*; he purchased the paper a few years later and styled it the *St. Joseph Valley Register*.

Schuyler Colfax, U.S. representative from Indiana, Speaker of the House of Representatives and the seventeenth vice president of the United States. *Library of Congress.*

Colfax was very active in the Whig Party, which he supported in his editorials and as a delegate to the party's convention in 1849 and the state constitutional convention in 1850. In 1851, Colfax secured a unanimous nomination as the Whig candidate for Congress but lost to the Democratic candidate. He did win election in 1853 and joined the Republican Party when the Whigs collapsed, and in 1862 he was elected Speaker of the House of Representatives.

Colfax was an earnest and energetic opponent of slavery yet briefly found a home in the virulently anti-Catholic and nativist Know-Nothing Party—which, with defected Whigs, Free-Soilers and Anti-Nebraska Act Democrats formed the Republican Party—and once railed against the "efforts of the Papal Church…to stride onward to commanding political power in this nation." Thus, it is curious that Father Sorin asserted in a wartime letter that Colfax was "an old friend" and that for twenty years they had been "if not intimates, at least very good acquaintances."[143]

To be sure, the University of Notre Dame was a significant economic presence in Colfax's home district; Father Sorin's biographer suggested that Colfax "found it expedient to muffle his distaste [for Catholics] and maintain amicable relations." Still, the biographer chided Father Sorin—"usually a good judge of people and their motivations"—for "foolishly" falling for Colfax's overtures. For his part, Colfax was counting on his "old friend" for the important elections in 1864.[144]

ALL POLITICS IS LOCAL

In the midterm elections of 1862—a tough proposition for the party in power—Colfax had faced stiff competition from Democrat "Dirty Dave" Turpie and won the election by a slim margin of fewer than three hundred votes. Now, even as the powerful Speaker of the House, Colfax faced another difficult election at home. The voting public's anxiety over wartime inflation and a burgeoning fifth column of Copperheads in Indiana compelled Colfax to write Lincoln that "the odds are heavy against us in Indiana." Colfax would again face Turpie, who was still stinging from his close defeat in 1862, which the Democrats attributed to "fraud and trickery." So motivated was Turpie to "lay Schuyler Colfax upon the shelf" that he turned down his party's nomination as lieutenant governor.[145]

On the eve of the election, Father Sorin wrote a friend: "[Colfax] is devoted to me, and, for the general well-being, I sometimes avail myself of this good will." He boasted again of the power he had related to the journalist Nichols, writing, "[Colfax] knows that I have at my disposal from sixty to seventy-five votes here [at Notre Dame] each election, either for him or against him." Colfax, who had always counted on those votes from Notre Dame, *needed* them in 1864. To that end, he visited Father Sorin to express his anxiety over the political landscape and reminded the good father of the draft exemptions and other political favors the Republican Party had secured for him.[146]

Father Sorin understood Colfax's not-so-subtle intimations and called a meeting of the priests and brothers that lasted for several hours and resulted in "a resolution which was calculated to have the best result"—that "no other ticket than the Republican or Union ticket shall be voted by the Members of the Congregation on tomorrow." Unfortunately, the person responsible for passing on this important information to the other members of the Notre Dame community failed to carry out this critical assignment, and the result was that—as Father Sorin reported to his superior—"three-fourths...voted against [Colfax]."[147]

Father Sorin attributed the vote against Colfax to ethnic politics, explaining that "most of the Irish in this country imagine, right or wrong, that the Republican Party is hostile to them." The reasons made little difference to Colfax, even though the Speaker had won his election by a comfortable margin. "He and his friends were indignant," Father Sorin reported, adding that "[our] house was very seriously compromised in the eyes of the country." The next month, Colfax conspired to recall the exemption that Father Carrier had obtained for the brothers on whom the draft had fallen, the Notre Dame post office was threatened and other privileges were under fire as well.[148]

Father Sorin then turned to prayer—every member of the community "promised to say one thousand Hail Marys," he recalled—but also to the "bold initiative" of sending Father Carrier back to Washington to plead with the War Department. In the end, as Father Sorin explained, it was prayer and *another* person's "bold initiative"—that of Ellen Sherman, wife of General William T. Sherman—that saved the day:

> *She took a lively interest in the case of the five conscripts, and wrote immediately to President Lincoln and Secretary of War Stanton. Providentially those letters were received in Washington on the very day when the general telegraphed to the government the fall of Savannah. It seems evident that the Blessed Virgin this time employed the excellent wife of the general to secure this favor.*[149]

Is the story of the timely intercession of Ellen Sherman's letters coincident with her husband's capture of Savannah too good to be true? Perhaps, yet at least one historian has expertly followed the paper trail and confirmed the story, which has become a staple of Notre Dame's mythology.[150]

Two years later, in the elections of 1866, Father Sorin apparently had exercised more control over the votes in his pocket, as Colfax graciously wrote:

> *I cannot let the election pass by without thanking you earnestly for the aid you rendered therein, and the majority that was thus given me in your township, generally so heavy the other way. I assure you I shall never forget it, and hope always to be worthy of the confidence you and your brethren have thus expressed.*[151]

Chapter 9
THE VALLEY OF
THE SHADOW

In war or in peace, one sees the epitome of man's existence in these few words: "he lived; he died." Hence men exposed to the dangers everywhere found in soldier life should always be ready to die.

−*Father William Corby*

Notre Dame's student-soldiers, priests and sister-nurses could be forgiven for being war-weary by 1864. Perhaps many of them were beginning to face their own mortality, as former student Orville T. Chamberlain, commanding a company of the 74th Indiana Infantry, expressed in a sobering letter to his family:

Dear Father:

Give each member of the family some souvenir by which they may remember me. You will find among my papers, if they have not been disturbed, one or two packages, bearing inscriptions to this effect: "In case of my death destroy these without reading," which please do.

You have ever been to me a good, kind, faithful father. I <u>tried</u> to be a good son, but did not succeed as well as I ought, or as well as I could wish. You have been at once to me father, friend and brother.

Mother and all the children: Forgive my errors, and any harsh words I have ever spoken to you.

Children, be good, mind your parents, be studious, be pious.

Orville[152]

Despite the Union victories at Gettysburg and Vicksburg in 1863, there were still two years of hard fighting to do, and Notre Dame men would remain in the thick of it.

MORE THAN BLOOD AND THUNDER

In the early months of 1864, Father William Corby and the soldiers and officers of the Irish Brigade returned to their camps on the north bank of the Rappahannock River in Virginia after a brief but well-deserved winter furlough in New York City. He and his dear friend Father Thomas Ouellet, a Jesuit priest who had shared the chaplain duties in the brigade, "put [their] heads together…to plan out the spiritual work for the coming campaign," much as the generals were doing themselves.[153]

Father Corby did not dwell much on his own mortality during the war; still, there were plenty of episodes in which he prepared other soldiers for their own deaths. Among the most touching are cases in which he prepared soldiers for their execution, the scenes of which "jarred my nerves much more than battle," he confessed years later. As a rule, he did not intrude on military justice but simply counseled the condemned men to fortify them before they faced the firing squad or noose. In April 1864, however, Father Corby did (unsuccessfully) intercede on one condemned soldier's behalf and even had an audience with President Abraham Lincoln in the process.[154]

Father Corby was with the Irish Brigade in the great battles of the eastern theater in 1864: The Wilderness, Spotsylvania Court House, Cold Harbor and the beginning of the long siege at Petersburg, Virginia. Father Corby did not write much of the battles themselves or his part in them, except to briefly mention that he ministered to the wounded and dying. His well-received memoir, written many years later, was purposely intended, he stated, to "give my readers…a notion of war life not entirely made up of 'blood and thunder' of the battlefield," but rather "the details of other trials and sufferings incurred by the poor soldier," including the mud, insects and incompetence, all with good humor.[155]

Father Corby was called back to Notre Dame in the fall of 1864 for school business, though it "required a positive order to tear him away from amidst the dangers that he had over and over again confronted without showing the least symptoms of fear," Father Sorin wrote. "My good long rest gave me fresh vigor," Father Corby remembered, and in early 1865 he returned to the army in its trenches around Petersburg. "I felt glad to be back again at the post of duty," Father Corby wrote, and he prepared the Irish Brigade for the campaign that would finally end the war.[156]

BATTLEFIELD PROMOTIONS

The naturally martial William Lynch was undoubtedly chafing to get back on the battlefield. Having been captured at Shiloh in April 1862 and released in October, it was early 1863 before he had the chance to recruit replacements for the 58th Illinois Infantry. He then commanded Camp Butler, a Union prisoner of war camp outside Springfield, Illinois, for several months in 1863. Lynch's oversight of Camp Butler—which held nearly two thousand Confederate prisoners—was competent but not exemplary. An inspector commented favorably on the accommodations, the rations and the keeping of the record books and accounts. Still, the inspector censured Lynch for the general condition of the camp and for the lack of discipline among the prisoners. His main complaint seemed to be that the camp was run with a strict—if "proper"—economy. No one specifically intimated that Lynch was retaliating for his own treatment at the hands of the Confederates, but the inspector did declare that Lynch, "who had been a prisoner in the South seemed to care only for the security of the prisoners" and paid no regard to the "[prisoners'] wants or comforts."[157]

In any event, the camp was closed in the summer of 1863, and by early 1864 Lynch—only twenty-four years old yet now commanding a brigade of three regiments—was once again ready for action. He joined the Red River Campaign of Union general Nathaniel P. Banks and participated in the March 14, 1864 capture of Fort De Russy, Louisiana. There he ordered an advance with fixed bayonets, and "with a yell that echoed through the timber" his brigade "sprang forward… and in less than ten minutes from the time the order was given to charge the stars and stripes waved in triumph" over the works of the fort. The auspicious start to the campaign was only temporary; a decisive Confederate victory at Mansfield, Louisiana, on April 8, 1864, turned the campaign into a retreat.[158]

A month later, at the Battle of Yellow Bayou, Louisiana, on May 18, 1864, a musket ball struck Lynch just below his knee as he was leading his brigade. Orderlies lifted Lynch from his horse and carried him away from the battlefield. While one surgeon, Dr. Lucas, dressed Lynch's leg, he assured him that the leg could be saved. Dr. Henry Crawford, Lynch's regimental surgeon, insisted that the leg must come off, but as Lucas outranked Crawford, his opinion held, and the leg was not amputated. For his part, Lynch maintained that it was his own medical opinion that held that day. "I had seen so many legs amputated without sufficient cause that I was determined not to lose mine," he told a Notre Dame professor after the war. "When they put me on the table, I gave my revolver to my orderly, and told him to shoot the surgeon if he tried to take off the leg."[159]

Fortunately for Lynch, another Notre Dame man was ready to take his place: Robert W. Healy. Healy, who entered Notre Dame in 1854 and graduated in 1859, was also active in the school's military company. In late 1861, Healy left his occupation to join the 58th Illinois, then being recruited by Lynch. He enlisted as a private but was soon elected captain of a company. He was with Lynch at Fort Donelson but was sick and missed the battle (and capture) at Shiloh. When the 58th Illinois was reorganized and back in action in 1864, so was Healy, and he assumed command of the regiment after Lynch was wounded and led it through the end of the war.

Lynch's corps commander at the Battle of Yellow Bayou, Major General Andrew J. Smith, was justly impressed with Lynch's leadership and courage under fire and wrote to the army's chief of staff, Henry W. Halleck, to press for a promotion:

Dec. 12, 1864

General—I have the honor to introduce to you hereby Col. Wm. F. Lynch...who has been serving for the past eighteen months in my command as regimental and brigade commander.

He entered the service in April, 1861, as a private, and afterward raised the Fifty-eighth Illinois, and was mustered into service with it December 20, 1861. Since that time he has been in the battles of Fort Donelson, Shiloh (where he was captured, after a heavy loss in officers and men), Fort De Russy, Pleasant Hill, and Yellow Bayou, La., in which last battle he was severely wounded in the leg while cheering his men to the charge.

As regimental and brigade commander he has few equals in energy, decision, and tact in the service; as an officer he is cool and courageous, and as a gentleman courteous and refined. His services and ability entitle him to a higher position than the one which he now holds, and I earnestly recommend that he be appointed brigadier-general of volunteers as an act of justice and policy.[160]

William Lynch's war ended at the Battle of Yellow Bayou, but he did eventually earn a promotion to brigadier general, as did his Notre Dame classmate and comrade in arms Robert W. Healy. Unfortunately, the decision on the part of Dr. Lucas not to amputate caused Lynch pain for the next dozen years and may have contributed to his death at the young age of thirty-seven in 1876.

Brave as a Lion

After the heavy fighting at Chickamuaga and Chattanooga in late 1863, Father Cooney and the 35th Indiana, like Father Corby and the Irish Brigade, got a well-deserved veteran's furlough after reenlisting *en masse* in mid-December 1863. Father Cooney went home to Monroe, Michigan, to visit his family and then returned to Tennessee in February 1864, where the regiment went into camp waiting for the next campaign. Father Cooney wrote to his brother that he was "very busy preparing the men to complete their Easter duty" and happily reported that thousands of non-Catholics attended his services and that "prejudice against the Church is gone almost entirely." An artist in the brigade "took the picture" of the Easter celebration and had a handsome engraving made in which Father Cooney is featured celebrating Mass; the corners of the print portrayed vignettes of the intrepid chaplain in action, including his attention to wounded soldiers on the battlefield.[161]

"Another battle is expected in a short time," Father Cooney wrote home in late April 1864, and he was right. Of the fighting that began in early May and lasted through late July, Father Cooney wrote his brother: "We have driven the rebel army nearly one hundred and fifty miles back and are fighting every mile…They run and we follow a few miles farther, and so it goes." Father Cooney and the 35th Indiana witnessed heavy battles. At Kennesaw Mountain on June 20, 1864, the regiment was engaged in hand-to-hand fighting, and its commander, Major John P. Duffey, was killed. On July 4, 1864, near Marietta, the unit charged and

This print, fashioned after a photograph, features Father Peter P. Cooney holding a church service for soldiers in the field, with vignettes of Father Cooney giving soldiers communion, a battle scene and sisters in the field hospital. *Library of Congress.*

captured a line of Confederate breastworks under a withering fire from both flanks. It also took an active part in the battles at Jonesboro and Lovejoy Station.[162]

"My three years will be expired the 4th day of October [1864]…and I have concluded not to stay any longer in the army," Father Cooney wrote to his brother in late July 1864. In another letter, he expressed his weariness, writing, "When I left home I did not think I would be so long in the army." Yet leaving the regiment would not be easy for him. "My parting with my nearest and dearest relatives, I would regard as nothing compared with the difficulty of parting with them," Father Cooney wrote home, adding, "To say the word 'farewell,' will be one of the hardest trials of my life." That fall, the army was once again on the move, and Father Cooney stayed with them, stating that "I could not think of leaving my brave fellows in the face of the enemy without a priest—not knowing what day a battle would be fought."[163]

Those battles would come but weeks later: at Franklin, Tennessee, on November 30, 1864, and at Nashville on December 15–16, 1864. Of the action, Father Cooney wrote, "I passed through two of the most terrible battles...All acknowledge there was no harder fighting during the war." Once again, Father Cooney earned official recognition for his bravery on the battlefield. In an official report, the division commander praised him as one "who remained in the front with his regiment, encouraging and cheering the men by his words and acts." Likewise, the brigade commander declared that Father Cooney was "brave as a lion" as he "worked with his brave regiment in the valley of the shadow of death, affording the ministrations of his holy religion to the wounded and dying and giving words of encouragement to his fellow soldiers."[164]

Father Cooney had already confessed that it would be hard to leave his regiment. Likewise, the men of the 35th Indiana were loath to lose their beloved chaplain and wrote a heartfelt petition to Father Sorin asking that Father Cooney be allowed to remain. They first expressed their gratitude "to Notre Dame and its Superior for the blessings of Father Cooney's ministry" and then added:

> Could we take you in imagination through our various camps which he converted for us into sanctuaries...and through the many scenes of privation, hardships, and bloodshed that his sacred ministry sanctified for us, you could then understand the strength of the ties that bind us to him and would surely pardon us for thus troubling you with our fears to face the thousand dangers that threaten us in his loss.
>
> His fidelity to his regiment and his untiring devotedness to his sacred ministry have become proverbial in the Army...The records of Father Cooney's many deeds of charity and Christian heroism have gained for him, in the Army of the Cumberland, an influence which he knows how to use...Our regiment is one of the largest in this army and presents of itself a wide field in which he had planted the seeds of Union harmony and Christian charity.
>
> If our Regiment can still lay claim to your love...we would humbly and earnestly press our petition...in the names of the souls his sacred ministry may yet rescue and in the name of our National Government that is now nearly past the ordeal that has tested its existence.[165]

"This document is a real masterpiece of the noblest sentiments of the human heart," Father Sorin commented soon after receiving it, adding that "the General of the division…with his own hand declared that the recall of F. Cooney 'would be a calamity.'" Father Sorin could not resist the petition. "Fr. Cooney could nowhere else be more highly esteemed, more loved, in a better position to do good," he wrote, and so Father Cooney remained with his regiment for the remainder of the war.[166]

AGAIN BLESSED WITH PEACE

Following his heroics at Chickamauga in September 1863, Orville T. Chamberlain settled into camp and prepared for the coming spring and summer campaign in Georgia. The hard fighting that ensued once again had Chamberlain contemplating his mortality. "I avail myself to let you know I am still in existence," he wrote home in early July 1864. "I have perfect confidence in the ability of the army to capture Atlanta. I may be killed in the attempt, but I firmly believe that the result so much to be desired will soon be accomplished." Still, he also earnestly hoped "that the day is not too far distant when our land will be again blessed with peace." To that end, Chamberlain began to plan his future, writing to his father that he was considering making a career of the army. He also explained why he had "new…(and powerful) incentives to be a man": "I love Dora [Isadore Ellis of Lafayette, Indiana] as fervently and as purely as ever and the many good, long, noble letters which I receive from her contain ample assurance that her affection for me is undiminished…[she] is a noble girl. I only wish that I deserved her love."[167]

After the long and brutal but successful Atlanta campaign, Chamberlain was promoted to captain, and a fellow Notre Dame classmate, John Schutt, was promoted to adjutant in the same regiment. Camped just outside Savannah, Georgia, Chamberlain often had opportunities to take dinner and share a night's entertainment with families in the area. That familiarity served him well for his important role in a thrilling raid that took place in November 1864. Early that month, thirty-one Union soldiers on a foraging detail—including several from the company that Chamberlain commanded—were captured by Confederate guerilla cavalry who had earned a reputation for murdering prisoners. The next day, under direct and urgent orders from General Sherman, Chamberlain led an advance guard of his regiment to secure the release of the prisoners or to wreak havoc on the local citizenry presumed to be implicated in the raid.

Chamberlain wrote that he "searched every house and arrested every man in the vicinity of the occurrence." Furnished with some intelligence before he set out on the expedition, Chamberlain boasted that he "added to our stock by 'pumping' our prisoners" by pretending to have lived in the area and inquiring about families he knew by name. In doing so, he learned the whereabouts of the expedition's principal target, Captain James M. Hendricks, the leader of the band of irregulars. Chamberlain "had the happiness of arresting [Hendricks] and relieving him of two splendid revolvers." When Chamberlain and his commander returned to headquarters, they were ushered into General Sherman's private room, where, as Chamberlain wrote, "he shook hands with us" and congratulated them on the successful expedition.[168]

On April 9, 1865, the Confederate Army of Northern Virginia—commanded by General Robert E. Lee—surrendered to Union commander General Ulysses S. Grant. Orville Chamberlain wrote to his father that they heard General Sherman's order announcing the surrender and that his camp "was full of excitement and joy." Still, his own war was not over yet, and he wrote that the same day they "had quite a brisk skirmish…Several shells and a great many bullets passed through our Regiment and we got close enough to the Rebels to see them."[169]

Within days, Chamberlain and his comrades also received the announcement of President Lincoln's assassination "with feelings of mingled rage and sorrow." They had all wanted to see Lincoln "live to see the fruits of his labors and we wanted to honor in the future his honesty and wisdom," and had the perpetrator of the "damnable deed" been in their midst, "he would be torn into a thousand tatters," Chamberlain declared. He then quoted what he thought to be suitable lines from Shakespeare's *Macbeth*:

> *Besides, this Duncan Hath borne his faculties so meek,*
> *He was so clear in his great office,*
> *that his virtues plead like angels, trumpet-tongued,*
> *against the deep damnation of his taking-off…*[170]

Chamberlain added: "We received Gen. Sherman's [order] announcing a suspension of hostilities and that there is a probability of a restoration of Peace. So it is probable that I will live to get home." On April 25, 1865, Confederate general Joseph E. Johnston surrendered to Union general William T. Sherman at Bennett Place, North Carolina. The war was over.[171]

Chapter 10

LET US HAVE PEACE

Life is only another kind of battle and it requires as good a generalship to conduct it to a successful end as it did to conquer a city, or to march through Georgia.
—William T. Sherman, Notre Dame commencement address, 1865

The Sherman family—fresh from grand reviews and a series of congratulatory banquets—stopped at Notre Dame on Wednesday, June 7, 1865. The university took advantage of the presence of their distinguished guest and invited him to speak at that day's commencement exercises. When Sherman entered the refectory, the students gave him an ovation. Timothy Howard, the wounded veteran of Shiloh—and now a Notre Dame professor—addressed the general on behalf of the faculty. The professor first congratulated Sherman on his military exploits and success and then on the general's special connection to the university:

> *We are glad that you have kindly visited us on your way; we knew you would not forget us. From the field of strife and the march, your heart must have often turned to the quiet shades where dwelt the treasures of your soul. And when the war was over, we knew that General Sherman would come to see the places made sacred to him by the consecrating footsteps of his family, and rest with us and let Notre Dame be a gentle spot in the midst of toils in the present and honors in the future.* [172]

Tommy Corcoran, a senior from Cincinnati, also congratulated the general and spoke with pride of how the university had a part in the

Union victory, stating that "[p]riests, sisters, professors and students have gone out from their quiet places, and have become part in your grand armies; and a feeling of glory goes up in our souls as we remember that we, too, have a share in your renown."[173]

The general's nephew, Tom Ewing, then spoke on behalf of the junior department. He first poked fun at the seniors, saying that most of them were going to be doctors so that they could "kill other people without endangering their own lives," while the rest would become lawyers so that they "may be smart enough to find excuses for avoiding all coming drafts." His fellow juniors, though, he proudly declared, "have unanimously and solemnly resolved...to be soldiers...[and] Major Generals, also." He then alluded touchingly to the general's favorite son, stating, "You have come here, we know, to visit the halls where Willy studied, the groves where he played, and the boys who were his friends—a title we are proud to claim."[174]

The general was deeply moved and assured the audience that the boys at Notre Dame were dear to him. Sherman declared that, under the circumstances, he would rather "fight a respectable battle in behalf of the nation's rights, than make a speech now," adding, "[b]ut it is clear that you expect me to say something and I don't want to disappoint you." He then delivered some unprepared remarks (his trademark), commenting on his own youth and the need for self-reliance and referring often to the great national struggle:

> *Let me not forget that I was once a young man like those who have appeared before the audience on this day and occasion. You should be grateful that you are under such good instruction and guidance. You now have a pilot on board to guide you, but the time will come, and soon, when you will have to go forth into the great, dark seas alone, under your own guidance...*
>
> *You must see to it that the ship is strong, the pilot true and the compass unerring....No one can tell when the ship might be wanted, when it will be required to go into action and even to do fighting for America. God knows there has been enough of fighting for a long spell, but it is the highest wisdom and the best policy...to be ready for that encounter at any moment...*
>
> *But I ask you to remember that, although I have no more than ordinary abilities such as any of you possess, I had not forgotten to take care of the ship and that I trusted in the pilot—in myself. I relied upon*

my own courage and foresight and in my devotion to the good old cause, to the Union, to truth, to liberty and, above all, to the God of battles…

So I call upon the young men here to be ready to at all times to perform bravely the battle of life…A young man should always stand in his armor, with his sword in hand and his buckler on.

The general concluded by promising the young men assembled that he would "always regard you and your pursuits with interest," with confidence that "each of you will try to make your careers honorable as well as successful," and then he then bade them farewell.[175]

NEW LIVES AND NEW ARRIVALS

With the war over and peace at hand, the erstwhile Notre Dame student-soldiers scattered across the country and began families and careers. The Holy Cross army chaplains and sister-nurses returned to Notre Dame, taking on new responsibilities. Father Corby succeeded Father Sorin as president of the university. Father Cooney became pastor of a local church before engaging in twenty-five years of missionary work. After many years at Notre Dame, Father Carrier was assigned as a professor at St. Laurent College, near Montreal, and expertly tended the natural history museum there for many years. In their spare time, such as it was, both Father Cooney and Father Corby interested themselves in veterans' affairs and writing war-related memoirs.

Other Civil War veterans also found their way to the university, specifically into Father Sorin's Holy Cross flock. "It is not strange… that after the war not a few of the disbanded soldiers and officers found their way as priests and brothers into the ranks of the Community, the heroism of whose members they had admired on the field and in the hospital," offered the school newspaper as way of explanation for the new arrivals. Typical was Brother Leander (James McLain), who entered the Congregation of the Holy Cross in 1872. Born in Pottsville, Pennsylvania, in 1842, he served through three years of the Civil War with the 15th United States Infantry as a private and was engaged at the Battles of Chickamauga, Chattanooga and Atlanta. Brother Leander was prefect of one of the halls and taught classes for many years at the university.[176]

Brother Sebastian (Thomas Martin) was said to have been wounded seven or eight times during the war when fighting with the 1st Pennsylvania

Cavalry. When, with Brother Leander's assistance, he sought a pension many years later, he carried a testimonial from his former commander, who wrote, "If old Tom is alive yet he, above all, deserves a pension. When Gen. Cobb of the Confederates was doing destructive work on our left flank I ordered Tom to dismount and rest his piece on my shoulder and aim at Gen. Cobb. This he did, and the General fell."[177]

Others included:

Brother Cosmas (Nicholas A. Bath)—2nd United States Artillery
Brother Raphael (James C. Maloy)—133rd Pennsylvania infantry
Brother Eustachius (John McInerny)—83rd Ohio Infantry
Brother Benedict (James Mantle)—1st Pennsylvania Heavy Artillery
Brother Ignatius (Ignatz Mayer)—75th and 157th Pennsylvania Infantry
Brother Agatho (Joseph Staley)—8th Indiana Infantry
Brother Richard (William Stoney)—38th New Jersey Infantry
Brother Polycarp (James White)—United States Navy

One of the most interesting stories is that of Mark A. Wills, who took the name of Brother John Chrysostom. Wills had fought with the 54th Pennsylvania, a unit that saw significant action in the eastern theater during the last year of the Civil War, including the Battle of New Market, the capture of Fort Gregg and the pursuit of Lee to Appomattox, where the 54th was captured in the last week of the war (though released a few days later). In at least one of those fights, Wills was sufficiently shaken to make a battlefield vow, which he related to Father Sorin in a letter many years later:

Very Rev. Dear Father

Just as I wrote the date of this letter I remembered on this day 24 years ago about this time in the morning I was in line of battle awaiting the charge. [We] were being shelled at the time and I heard in a clear and distinct voice "[You] will be killed today." I knew it was no human voice and I was perfectly convinced of the certainty of death. I prayed fervently as I never prayed before to our sweet Mother that if She would intercede for me and get me out safe that I would [surely] delay no longer in responding to the call that was continually urging me to apply to some religious community for admission. I had hardly concluded my prayer when the same voice said "You will only be hurt today" and it happened so…only that I delayed 3 years or rather 2 years after the war in fulfilling my promise when I enlisted under the banner of the Holy Cross."[178]

The most distinguished record among the new arrivals belonged to William A. Olmsted. Born in Albany, New York, in 1834, Olmsted received his MD from Howard University. When the Civil War broke out in 1861, he raised one of the state's first volunteer companies for the 2nd New York Infantry and was elected captain; he quickly earned a promotion to lieutenant colonel. He then served as commander of the 59th New York Infantry and a brigade commander in the Army of the Potomac, where he was brevetted a brigadier general of volunteers. After the war, Olmsted served in a medical capacity in the forts on the upper Missouri River, where he became close to (and respected by) the Sioux in his care. Olmsted then entered the Holy Cross community at Notre Dame in the 1890s, studied for the priesthood and was ordained in 1901.

WE HAPPY FEW, WE BAND OF BROTHERS

In the autumn of 1897, the remaining Civil War veterans in the classrooms and halls of Notre Dame decided to join the ranks again, this time by forming their own post—a very special one, in fact—of the country's most active Union veterans' organization, the Grand Army of the Republic (GAR). "In no other country in the world is there to be found a more interesting and unique aggregation of battle-scarred veterans than those forming the very latest post to be added to the Grand Army of the Republic," a newspaper reported that fall. Besides the notable personalities, Notre Dame's chapter—Post No. 569—was unique because it was the only one in the country composed entirely of ordained priests or professed religious men as members.[179]

On the evening of October 5, 1897, the Auten Post members of the GAR of nearby South Bend, Indiana, marched in a body from their homes and filed into Washington Hall on campus for the inaugural ceremonies. The university band played a march as the enthusiastic crowd that had waited outside the hall began to enter. Father Peter P. Cooney—installed as chaplain of the new post—offered a heartfelt and patriotic prayer, begging God's grace to "infuse into the hearts of our

University of Notre Dame Grand Army of the Republic Post 569. *University of Notre Dame Archives.*

members the spirit of charity to carry out the main objects of the Post: to aid one another in sickness and misfortune and to foster the spirit of true patriotism by which love for our glorious Union and Constitution may be daily increased in the hearts of all."[180]

Father William Corby—elected commander—then gave a welcoming address followed by additional speeches given by visiting dignitaries. The formal part of the ceremony being over, the balance of the evening was given to sharing war stories and tales of amusement. General St. Clair Mulholland, Father Corby's old friend and comrade in the Irish Brigade—who had come eight hundred miles to attend—obliged by giving an address full of good Irish humor. "One principal object of the Grand Army is to keep alive the recollections of the war," he declared, and then told the following story (among many that night):

On our march to Petersburg I came upon two Irishmen enjoying a chat. I had nothing else to do and listened to their conversation. One of the

Irishman said: "Barney, I don't know what the divil brought ye here. I knew ye in New York when ye were in the grocery business and doin' first rate. Why ye came out here I don't know." "Why," said he, "Mike, I'll tell ye why I came here. I am a married man and came to war to have peace."

"Why the members of this post went to war I don't know. They certainly had no such reason as that," Mulholland concluded in a friendly jab at his celibate hosts.[181]

The evening concluded with the reading of telegrams of congratulation from around the country (the new post had received attention in newspapers from St. Louis to Chicago, Cleveland, Newark and more) and a closing address from Father Morrissey, president of Notre Dame, who declared his own pride in the school's Civil War record and who hoped that "every student of the University who is present will draw from these exercises the lessons of true patriotism that will be an inspiration to him in time to come to do his duty as the privileged son of a privileged land."[182]

While the veteran sister-nurses at St. Mary's couldn't join in the night's revelry or comradeship at Post No. 569, they kept alive and celebrated the memories of their service in their own special way. The singing of an adaptation of an old war song, "Tenting Tonight on the Old Campground," became an annual ritual as the sisters departed for summer missionary work:

We are tenting to-night on the dear home ground,
Give us a song to cheer,
A song of hope for our eager hearts,
And our path of duty clear.

Thinking of the days gone by.
Of the Vows we have made, and the love we must bear
Those Vows till the day we die.

We are waiting to-night on the old home ground;
But, our labors one day o'er,
We shall come to sleep 'neath the old home ground,
And shall part from home no more.[183]

Mustering Out

The priests and brothers of GAR Post No. 569 took detailed handwritten notes of their meetings: minutes were read and approved; the quartermaster delivered a treasurer's report; new eligible veterans in the Notre Dame community were found and welcomed to the post; veteran-priests from around the country—intrigued by the unique nature of the post—asked to be counted in their number; badges were purchased; War Department headstones were ordered for Notre Dame priests and brothers who had already died; and some of the men were invited to take leadership positions at the state and national level, which was a great honor to themselves and to Notre Dame.

The minutes of the meeting on December 24, 1897, indicate that Father Corby was reelected commander for the coming year, with other new officers noted in turn. Five days later, the minutes read that the post had been "called together, in extraordinary special meeting, consequent on the death of Very Rev Wm. Corby, Commanding the Post. It was announced by the Senior Vice Commander [Brother Leander] that the death of our honored and greatly lamented Comrade Commander took place December 28, 1897." The veterans solemnly directed the quartermaster to order a headstone, elected a new commander (William Olmsted) and drafted a heartfelt resolution:

> *The Notre Dame Post No. 569...Grand Army of the Republic, has in the death of its Commander, the Very Rev. William Corby, C.S.C., sustained a loss...He was a noble soldier, ever ready at the call of his office to perform the duties of the Chaplain; fearless under every trial of life. Whether as a soldier in behalf of his country, or as a soldier of the cross, he has ever been ready to lift up the fallen, support the weak and sustain the strong.*

"We feel the loss so severely that we have hardly courage to pen our feelings," the veterans concluded.[184]

The university at once "put away the things of rejoicing and the pleasure of the holidays, and the halls were cast in gloom," and "in the corridors of the main building nearly everyone spoke in undertones" as Father Corby's body lay in state in the university parlor for two days. By the morning of the funeral, hundred of mourners had gathered to follow the casket as it wound through the campus, which was covered in snow.

The queue had quite a martial flair; it was led by the members of local GAR posts, and the casket was flanked by the cadets from the university's military company. After the last rites of the church had been sung, a last volley fired and a last call of the bugle sounded, the coffin—wrapped in the Stars and Stripes—was lowered into its grave.[185]

It was a ritual that would be repeated several times over in the coming years. Father Cooney died in May 1905 and was buried with military honors in the same fashion. Still, his fellow veteran priests and brothers in Notre Dame's GAR Post No. 569 continued to meet and conduct their business, but in time the campfires became less frequent and the minutes less copious, until they consisted of little more than annual ledgers of the very few members still living.

CONCLUSION

Rest on embalmed and sainted dead! Dear as the blood ye gave;
No impious footstep here shall tread The herbage of your grave;
Nor shall your glory be forgot While Fame her record keeps,
For honor points the hallowed spot Where valor proudly sleeps.
  — "Bivouac of the Dead," Theodore O'Hara

H is] quiet exit…casts a softly solemn shadow over Memorial Day," the editors of the *Notre Dame Scholastic* reported on the passing of Brother Raphael in their May 28, 1921 issue. They continued:

> *It foreshadows the Memorial Day not far distant when the last wrinkled veteran is mustered out of the Grand Army and the epic struggles of the Civil War will have become tradition. With the tender echoes of the bugle gently dying over the veteran's grave a radiant chapter in the history of Notre Dame was closed. With him went the last living link to vitalize the memory of the University in the Rebellion….And for that the death of Brother Raphael is doubly significant. It marks the last of an illustrious nobility and it was the departure of a noble man.*[186]

Brother Raphael was the last of his comrades of the Notre Dame GAR post to find his final rest in the congregation cemetery. The vast majority of the graves are marked by simple crosses; however, the members of the community who were chaplains, soldiers or nurses have a small marble footstone bearing a record of their service. Each Memorial Day, the Stars

Cemetery marker for Holy Cross Sister Francis de Sales showing that she served as a U.S. Army nurse. *Sisters of the Holy Cross Records and Archives.*

and Stripes are placed on the graves to commemorate the service the Holy Cross priests, brothers and sisters had given during the Civil War.

Likewise, the parents of a former Notre Dame student built a memorial to their fallen son, fellow soldiers honored their favorite Notre Dame chaplain in bronze and grateful citizens saw to it that the sacrifices and mercy of the Holy Cross sister-nurses would not be forgotten. Thus, testaments to the epic story of Notre Dame in the Civil War can be found, from the country's capital city to an Indiana town to the battlefield at Gettysburg.

THE TWO LADIES

Perhaps the most unusual (and earliest) of the memorials to Holy Cross community service in the Civil War were the twin captured Confederate cannons—named "Lady Polk" and "Lady Davis"—that found a home on the campus of St. Mary's. The guns were large experimental rifled cannon, each more than ten feet long, weighing more than seven tons and designed to fire solid shot that weighed more than one hundred pounds. The guns were placed in Rebel forts on the Mississippi River but fell into the hands of the Union navy in early 1862. Later in the year, Commodore W.H. Davis, commanding the Western Flotilla, wrote the following order:

> *I wish you to stop at Island No. 10 and take on board the fragments of a gun known as the Lady Davis, which burst in the hands of the rebels. I wish you to stop again at Columbus and to take on board the fragments of a gun known as the Lady Polk, which also burst in the hands of the rebels…they are to be placed at the disposal of Sister Angela, superior of the Sisters of the Holy Cross, who are the principal nurses in our military hospitals, and that they are to be recast into a statue of peace for one of the religious establishments of which Sister Angela is the superior.*[187]

The cannons were delivered to Cairo, Illinois, in the care of Captain A.W. Pennock, who wrote to Mother Angela that he would "be very happy to keep here the guns…subject to any directions or orders which you may think proper to give me." The cannons were then transferred to the naval yard in Mound City, Illinois, where they remained for some time before finally finding their intended home at St. Mary's. They sat on the grounds under the flagpole flying the Stars and Stripes, and students often had their photos taken sitting on the "Ladies."[188]

In her 1881 collection *Crowned with Stars*, poet Eleanor C. Donnelly paid tribute to the sisters' wartime service and to their unique monument in "The Cannon in the Convent Grounds," which read in part:

> *O'er the cold metal, now rusty and rimy*
> *Year after year the green mosses have crept;*
> *Silvery sweet, thro' yon tubes dark and grimy*
> *The bells of St. Mary's their echoes have swept*

Come put your ear to these lips black and hoary
List to this voice, breathing ruin no more
The harsh tones grow sweet as they tell of the story
Of Mercy's blest part in the pageant of war

Lift the great guns from the snows that enfold them,
Heat the great furnace,—War's echoes must cease;
Swift in the might flames melt them and mould them
Into one image—Our Lady of Peace[189]

Mother Angela's original plans, put to rhyme by Donnelly, never came to pass: instead of being crafted into a monument of peace, the cannons actually went to war *again*. In September 1942, the sisters offered the guns to the government as salvage ore. Mr. L.J. Harwood—chairman of the Salvage Committee, Civilian Defense Council, St. Joseph County, Indiana—wrote to thank the sisters and St. Mary's Academy for their thoughtfulness:

I frequently have occasion to observe people who possess a tremendous amount of negative patriotism. That is, they are patriotic enough to give away some of their holdings if a large amount of pressure is put upon them. This gesture of yours, however, is quite different from this. I believe that you recognize that patriotism does not end until the object needed is finally secured. In this case the cannon are of no avail until they are melted, and if it had not been for your noble gesture, they probably would have remained on your campus until after the duration.[190]

The Sisters of the Holy Cross are also featured on the "Nuns of the Battlefield" monument in Washington, D.C., at the corner of Rhode Island Avenue and M Street Northwest, opposite St. Matthew's Church. The monument was the brainchild of Ellen Ryan Jolly, president of the Ladies' Auxiliary of the Ancient Order of Hibernians, an Irish Catholic fraternal organization. Long inspired by the stories she had heard of the contributions of sister-nurses during the Civil War, she petitioned the War Department in 1908 for a monument to their service. Told that she needed more documentation, Jolly spent a decade interviewing surviving sister-nurses and scouring archives. In 1921, Congress approved the monument with the proviso that it would not require government funds and that the design met the approval of the Commission of Fine Arts.

The "Lady Polk" and "Lady Davis" cannons on the campus of St. Mary's Academy. *Sisters of the Holy Cross Records and Archives.*

The Ladies' Auxiliary, led by Jolly, raised $50,000 and selected sculptor Jerome Connor—already famous for his Irish and Catholic statuary in the city—to design the monument. The commission approved Connor's design in 1919 (after much back and forth), and the monument was dedicated in a ceremony in September 1924. The large bas relief—six feet high and nine feet wide—includes life-size figures of women wearing the habits of the twelve orders that contributed nurses during the war, including the Sisters of the Holy Cross. Large bronze angels—of Peace and Patriotism—sit on either end. An inscription reads: "They comforted the dying, nursed the wounded, carried hope to the imprisoned, gave in His name a drink of water to the thirsty."[191]

More than a century after the October night in 1861 when the Holy Cross sisters were first called as nurses, they continued to be memorialized. In 1963, the Indiana Civil War Centennial Commission erected a marker in South Bend to their service. In 1990, the Great Lakes Naval Center, near Chicago, invited the Sisters of the Holy Cross to attend the dedication of the aptly named USS Red Rover branch health clinic.

The "Nuns of the Battlefield" monument in Washington, D.C. *Craig Swain.*

A FITTING TRIBUTE

Silas Baldwin was one of the most esteemed citizens of Elkhart, Indiana. As a pioneer of northern Indiana, he attended a log cabin school, volunteered in the Blackhawk War, ran a general store, helped bring the railroad to Elkhart, served as the city's postmaster and retired as vice-president of the city's First National Bank, which he helped found. He was active in Democrat Party politics and was nominated twice for the state legislature; as one town history declared, "He changed his political views when Fort Sumter was fired upon and thereafter was a consistent Republican."[192]

Mr. Baldwin was also the father of Frank Baldwin, the teenager—formerly a student at Notre Dame—who was killed in action at the Battle of Stones River on the last day of 1862. As if that was not a sufficient sacrifice to place on the altar of the nation, Silas also lost one of his daughters, Helen Jane, wife of Colonel John W. Shaffer. When not traveling with her husband in the field, Helen volunteered as a nurse at the Jefferson (Indiana) General Hospital, one of the largest of the war. She contracted one of the many diseases rampant in the wards and died on July 24, 1865.

Silas Baldwin, "through his love for the Union cause in general and from a sense of his own great personal loss in connection with the great tragedy of the rebellion," had long sought to erect a monument to Elkhart's soldiers and sailors as a gift to the city. In 1888, the city established an association for that purpose, and Baldwin contributed $2,000; the committee proceeded with laying the foundation, at which time he asked to pay the entire expense of the monument, which ended up far exceeding the original designs and budget of the city. He selected the best of materials and witnessed the first carloads of Bedford marble—from quarries in his own state—arrive in Elkhart twenty-six years to the day after his son was killed on a battlefield in Tennessee.[193]

Nearly eight hundred cubic feet of stone were used for the pedestal and coping, in gigantic blocks of four to eight tons each. When finished, the monument was thirty-two feet high on four bases, the third of which contained the names Stone River, Shiloh, Atlanta and Appomattox. Three panels contained fitting quotes from James A. Garfield, Ulysses S. Grant, John A. Logan, Oliver P. Morton and Abraham Lincoln, and the fourth carried the dedication: "Erected by Silas Baldwin in honor of the heroes who fought and the martyrs who fell in the war of 1861–1865." The whole was surmounted with a life-size statue of an infantryman at rest, cast in solid bronze. Surely the most touching feature was an upper die with a medallion portrait of the fallen Frank Baldwin, cast in bronze, "copied and enlarged from a small card picture and…said to be a perfect likeness," with the place and date of his death. The monument was ready for a grand unveiling.[194]

"Main Street never got such a washing as was given it this morning by the firemen," the *Elkhart Review* declared from its pages on August 23, 1889. And with good cause: the monument dedication that day attracted citizens and dignitaries from near and far. Local shops closed early so their employees could witness the ceremonies; many of the city's businesses and residences were elaborately decorated and beautiful, "probably never having been surpassed here," the *Review* declared. "Elkhart can take care of large crowds…[and] has shown her ability to entertain great men today," the paper proudly added.[195]

Yet for the crowd that was present, one very important person was missing: Silas Baldwin. He had passed away in May, just three months short of the great dedication day. The Baldwin home was "marked by a good-sized flag displayed from an upper window." Portraits of Frank Baldwin, Silas Baldwin and George Washington were in the

The Elkhart (Indiana) Soldiers and Sailors Monument, commissioned by Mr. Silas Baldwin, father of fallen Notre Dame student-soldier Frank Baldwin. *Patrick Brownewell.*

windows as well. Among the "great men" in attendance that day was Governor Alvin P. Hovey, who delivered the dedication address. Other dignitaries spoke at length until, finally, Jeremiah Bowen—a local disabled veteran—pulled the veil, and "the air was rent with cheers by the throng which filled the street."[196]

"The city may well be proud of the gift that its generous friend [Silas Baldwin] bestowed, and it will see that the emotions that prompted it are kept sacred, and that the scenes and sorrows it recalls are held in holy remembrance," the editors of the *Review* promised. For years, streetcars and horse-drawn wagons plied past the monument, which stood at an intersection in the city's center. The advent of the automobile and increased traffic prompted the city fathers to move the monument to Elkhart's Rice Cemetery in 1923. In 1989, a century after the original dedication, the city set aside $16,000 (four times the original cost) to restore and rededicate the statue, thus keeping the *Review*'s promise.[197]

"Fair Catch Corby"

More than any other Notre Dame personality connected with the Civil War, Father William Corby has been the object of the just admiration of the public for almost 150 years. He has been immortalized in paintings, poetry, books and even modern film. Certainly the most enduring and most famous of these memorials is the statue of Father Corby on the battlefield at Gettysburg, a replica of which also stands on the campus of the University of Notre Dame.

Father Corby's comrade in the Irish Brigade, General St. Clair Mulholland, once commanding officer of the 116th Pennsylvania Infantry, first had the idea to commemorate the scene at Gettysburg when the chaplain gave his famous "Absolution Under Fire." Indeed, "idea" may be too slight a word; one writer called it Mulholland's "one great hope and one great ambition…to see his dearly beloved friend commemorated to a heroic status placed upon a rock on the site of the famous absolution." Despite his zeal, Mulholland's early efforts to raise funds fell on deaf ears and empty pockets. "I started the movement here by going to see some wealthy people, but I was so discouraged I gave it up," Mulholland wrote to Notre Dame administrators in late 1907. "The surviving officers and men of our faith throughout the country are poor. Hardly one of them has a cent," he lamented.[198]

Statue of Father Corby at Gettysburg National Military Park. A replica of the statue on the Notre Dame campus has earned the nickname "Fair Catch Corby." *Michael Aubrecht.*

However, Mulholland persisted. He had made a career of recounting the scene on the lecture circuit, and at a December 1908 meeting of the Federation of Catholic Societies, he was called once again to the platform to narrate the stirring episode. The next month, the Catholic Alumni Sodality of Philadelphia, inspired by his recent telling, resolved to erect "a bronze statue, of heroic mould...on the Battlefield at Gettysburg upon the natural pedestal of the great boulder whereon he actually stood at the moment of the memorable incident." This time, the fundraising effort—led by Mulholland—succeeded with the enthusiastic endorsements and contributions of the nation's Catholic hierarchy and influential laymen.[199]

The sodality commissioned Samuel Aloysius Murray to craft the statue. A native of Philadelphia, Murray began his artistic studies at the age of seventeen under the tutelage of the renowned American painter and sculptor Thomas Eakins. Murray was an ideal choice for the Father Corby statue: he had strong ties to Philadelphia's Irish Catholic community, and by the turn of the century he had become one of America's most promising artisans. His works won recognition at expositions in America and in Europe and are prominent in Philadelphia and Washington, D.C. His most ambitious piece, the *Goddess of Victory and Peace* atop the Pennsylvania State Memorial, shares the Gettysburg battlefield with his statue of Father Corby.

In 1910, Murray proceeded quickly with the model and with the final casting. The unveiling was scheduled for later in the year, but unfortunately—as with the Baldwin monument in Elkhart, Indiana— the Corby statue's greatest patron did not live to see the day. General Mulholland died on February 17, 1910. He literally worked on the statue until the day he passed, so concerned was he that his cherished project would fail; in the morning he had written a letter to the University of Notre Dame about the statue and—as Henry A. Daily, president of the sodality, remembered—"a few hours before [Mulholland] died, he sent for me and I then assured him that the monument need give him no concern as I felt that the erection of the monument…was as certain as if the statue was at that time in place."[200]

Trains began arriving in Gettysburg on Friday, October 28, 1910. That evening a "camp fire" was held in a town hall, where children from the local Catholic school sang songs such as "Tenting Tonight on the Old Camp Ground" and dignitaries such as University of Notre Dame president Father John Cavanaugh delivered speeches. By one o'clock on Saturday afternoon, as church bells rang, hundreds more visitors had arrived by train and had begun assembling on the battlefield (on Hancock Avenue) for the ceremony. Walter George Smith, a noted Philadelphia lawyer and master of ceremonies, declared:

We are assembled to commemorate an event unique in the history of the great Civil War…The pages of history glow with the records of deeds and heroism done on land and sea by officers, soldiers and sailors, who illustrated courage on both sides of the mighty conflict, and with fitting appreciation…the scenes they have immortalized have been marked by grateful people, but now for the first time a monument has been erected to perpetuate the memory of a deed done directly for the glory of God and the salvation of the human soul. Amid these triumphant monuments of soldiers we have placed the presentment of a priest...performing one of the most sacred functions of his office...We may hope that it will bring to the minds of every traveler upon this field for generations yet unborn...the name and deed of the heroic Chaplain.[201]

After additional speeches and a benediction, a young girl pulled a flag covering the bronze statue of Father Corby, hat and gloves at his feet, left hand over his heart and his right arm raised in absolution. "There was no attempt at ostentation or display," a local newspaper reported, "but as the folds of the Stars and Stripes dropped and revealed the figure of the revered father...the entire audience stood for a moment of silence in token of their regard, esteem and respect for the man whose memory was so fittingly honored today."[202]

The next summer, on Decoration Day (Memorial Day), 1911, a replica of the Gettysburg statue was unveiled on the campus of the University of Notre Dame in front of Corby Hall, "with an assemblage of exercises not often seen. Religion, eloquence, music, military display, a large audience and a perfect summer day added each a glory to the solemn event." The Notre Dame students, fond of renaming statues and paintings on campus as football-related icons—"Touchdown Jesus" and "We're Number One Moses" as examples—refer to the statue as "Fair Catch Corby" due to his upraised arm. One of Father Corby's modern biographers, noting that the priest was "always known for his genial good humor," concluded that "Father Corby would enjoy the joke."[203]

The Civil War story of the University of Notre Dame came full circle on the day the Corby statue was unveiled on campus in 1911, as reported by the school paper: "Following the ceremonies, students and visitors went to Brownson Hall...to witness the maneuvers of the military companies. Without any question the work of the battalion on this occasion surpassed all previous records."[204]

In only a few years' time, Notre Dame's history was again "shrouded by the mists of war." The university would once again send its loyal sons—more than a thousand—to fight and die, this time on battlefields half a world away.

NOTES

ABBREVIATIONS

IHS: Indiana Historical Society, Indianapolis, Indiana.

IPAC: Indiana Province Archives Center, Congregation of the Holy Cross, Notre Dame, Indiana.

NARA: National Archives and Records Administration, Washington, D.C.

OR: *The War of the Rebellion: A Compilation of the Official Records of the Union and Confederate Armies.* 128 vols. Washington, D.C.: Government Printing Office, 1880–1901.

UNDA: University of Notre Dame Archives, Notre Dame, Indiana.

INTRODUCTION

1. Letter, Orville Chamberlain to family, March 4, 1861, Joseph W. and Orville T. Chamberlain Papers (hereafter Chamberlain Papers), Box 1, Folder 8, IHS.

CHAPTER 1

2. Edward Sorin, CSC, *The Chronicles of Notre Dame du Lac*, trans. William Toohey, ed. James T. Connelly (Notre Dame, IN: University of Notre Dame Press, 1992), 276.

3. Arthur J. Hope, *Notre Dame: One Hundred Years* (Notre Dame, IN: University Press, 1948), 116; *A Brief History of the University of Notre Dame du Lac, Indiana from 1842 to 1892* (Chicago, IL: Werner Co., 1895), 93.

4. *Chicago Daily Times*, October 4, 1858, quoted in *St. Joseph County Forum*, October 16, 1858, 3.

5. *Notre Dame Scholastic*, November 18, 1899, 175; January 13, 1872, 5.

6. Hope, *Notre Dame*, 117; Financial Ledger 4 (ULDG/4), 1859–60, 335, UNDA.

7. Letter, Neal Gillespie to mother, October 30, 1859, in Thomas Ewing Manuscripts (CEWI), Box 3, UNDA.

8. *St. Joseph County Forum*, June 18, 1859, 1.

9. Letter, Neal Gillespie to mother, April 19, 1861, CEWI, Box 3, UNDA.

10. Timothy E. Howard, *A History of St. Joseph County, Indiana*, vol. 2 (Chicago, IL: Lewis Publishing Co., 1907), 716; *Notre Dame Scholastic*, November 18, 1899, 176.

11. *Notre Dame Scholastic*, November 18, 1899, 176–77.

12. Ibid.

13. Howard, *History of St. Joseph County*, 637.

14. Oliver Jensen, "War Correspondent: 1864," *American Heritage* 31, no. 5 (August–September 1980): 48–64.

15. Ibid.

16. Ibid.

17. Hope, *Notre Dame*, 172; Letter, William A. Pinkerton to Andrew Morrissey, January 17, 1898, Notre Dame Presidents' Letters (UPEL), 65/04, UNDA.

18. Personal correspondence, Linda Fluharty to author, January 5, 2010.

19. Personal correspondence, Peter J. Lysy, UNDA, to author, January 15, 2010.

20. Michael Quinlan, Compiled Service Record (CSR), War Department Collection of Confederate Records (RG 109), M324, NARA.

21. Ibid.; personal correspondence, Linda Fluharty to author, January 5, 2010.

22. Personal correspondence, Peter J. Lysy, UNDA, to author, February 4, 2010.

23. Felix Zeringue, CSR, RG 109, M320, NARA; Felix Zeringue, Confederate Pension Application, Louisiana Secretary of State, Reel CP1.151, Microdex 4, Sequence 19.

CHAPTER 2

24. Robert J. Miller, *Both Prayed to the Same God: Religion and Faith in the American Civil War* (Lanham, MD: Lexington Books, 2007), 97.
25. Sorin, *Chronicles of Notre Dame du Lac*, 276.
26. David P. Conyngham, "Soldiers of the Cross," David Power Conyngham Papers (CCON), 1/08 (un-paginated typescript), UNDA.
27. Letter, Paul E. Gillen to Sorin, September 14, 1861, IPAC.
28. Ibid.; Conyngham, "Soldiers of the Cross."
29. Letter, Francis Patrick Kenrick to Sorin, October 15, 1861, IPAC; Letter, James F. Wood to Sorin, October 18, 1861, IPAC; Marvin R. O'Connell, *Edward Sorin* (Notre Dame, IN: University of Notre Dame Press, 2001), 455.
30. Letter, Kenrick to Sorin, November 25, 1861, IPAC; Conyngham, "Soldiers of the Cross."
31. William Corby, *Memoirs of Chaplain Life: Three Years with the Irish Brigade in the Army of the Potomac*, ed. Lawrence F. Kohl (New York: Fordham University Press, 1992), 286.
32. Ibid., 291.
33. Conyngham, "Soldiers of the Cross."
34. Sorin, *Chronicles of Notre Dame du Lac*, 292–93.
35. "Obituary of Rev. J.M.Z. Leveque," *New York Herald* clipping, February 14, 1862, Lévêque File, IPAC.
36. Conyngham, "Soldiers of the Cross."
37. Ibid.
38. Thomas McAvoy, "The War Letters of Father Peter Paul Cooney of the Congregation of the Holy Cross," *Records of the American Catholic Historical Society of Philadelphia*, vol. 44 (1933), 54–55.
39. Corby, *Memoirs of Chaplain Life*, 11.
40. Ibid., xxi.

CHAPTER 3

41. "Females Not Suitable for Nurses," *American Medical Times* (July 18, 1861): 30; John H. Brinton, *Personal Memoirs of John H. Brinton* (New York: Neale Publishing Co., 1914), 44.

42. *A Story of Fifty Years: From the Annals of the Congregation of the Sisters of the Holy Cross, 1855–1905* (Notre Dame, IN: Ave Maria, 1905), 90.

43. Anna S. McAllister, *Flame in the Wilderness: Life and Letters of Mother Angela Gillespie, C.S.C., 1824–1887* (Paterson, NJ: St. Anthony Guild Press, 1944), 170–71.

44. Ibid., 171.

45. Sister M. Paula Casey, Civil War nursing reminisces, typescript from handwritten document, Archives and Records of the Congregation of the Sisters of the Holy Cross, Notre Dame, Indiana (hereafter ARCSHS).

46. Mary A.R. Livermore, *My Story of the War: A Woman's Narrative of Four Years Personal Experience* (Hartford, CT: A.D. Worthington, 1890), 204.

47. Brinton, *Personal Memoirs*, 44–45.

48. *On the King's Highway: A History of the Sisters of the Holy Cross—Notre Dame, Indiana* (New York: D. Appleton & Co., 1931), 248.

49. Livermore, *My Story of the War*, 218.

50. Casey, ARCSHS.

51. E. Kent Loomis, "History of the U.S. Navy Hospital Ship *Red Rover*," Navy Department, Office of the Chief of Naval Operations, Division of Naval History, Ships' History Section, Report No. OP 09B9, 1961, 7.

52. Mary D. Maher, *To Bind Up the Wounds: Catholic Sister Nurses in the U.S. Civil War* (Baton Rouge: Louisiana State University Press, 1999), 91.

53. Barbara M. Wall, "Grace Under Pressure: The Nursing Sisters of the Holy Cross, 1861–1865," *Nursing History Review* 1 (1993): 80.

54. *Harper's Weekly*, "The Naval Hospital Boat 'Red Rover,'" May 9, 1863, 299.

55. Livermore, *My Story of the War*, 219.

56. Sarah H. Emerson, ed., *Life of Abby Hopper Gibbons* (New York: G.P. Putnam's Sons, 1897), 348; Livermore, *My Story of the War*, 218–19.

57. *On the King's Highway*, 238.

58. *A Story of Fifty Years*, 100.

CHAPTER 4

59. O'Connell, *Edward Sorin*, 453.

60. Sorin, *Chronicles of Notre Dame du Lac*, 279.

61. *Report of the Adjutant General of the State of Illinois*, vol. 4 (Springfield, IL: Phillips Bros., 1901), 107.

62. *OR*, ser. 1, vol. 10, pt. I, 164–65.

63. *Elgin Weekly Gazette*, "From the 58th," July 23, 1862.

64. *History of St. Joseph County, Indiana* (Chicago, IL: Chas. C. Chapman, 1880), 645.

65. Timothy E. Howard, *Musings and Memories* (Chicago, IL: Lakeside Press, 1905), 38–41.

66. O'Connell, *Edward Sorin*, note in photo following page 526.

67. Corby, *Memoirs of Chaplain Life*, 32.

68. Ibid., 64–65; *OR*, ser. 1, vol. 11, pt. I, 778.

69. Corby, *Memoirs of Chaplain Life*, 72.

70. Ibid., 82–84.

71. Ibid., 85, 131–32, 134–35.

72. David Stevenson, *Indiana's Roll of Honor*, vol. 1 (Indianapolis, IN: A.D. Streight, 1864), 565.

73. Ibid., 562–63.

74. McAvoy, "War Letters of Father Peter Paul Cooney," 152.

75. Ibid.; *OR*, ser. 1, vol. 20, pt. I, 612.

76. *Elkhart (IN) Review*, August 23, 1889, 2–3.

77. Ibid.

78. Ibid.

CHAPTER 5

79. John F. Marszalek, *Sherman: A Soldier's Passion for Order* (New York: Free Press, 1993), 6.

80. Letter, Ellen Sherman to William T. Sherman, August 17, 1862, William T. Sherman Family Papers (hereafter CSHR), 2/99, UNDA.

81. Letter, Maria Sherman to William T. Sherman, June 27, 1862, CSHR 2/99, UNDA.

82. Letter, Ellen Sherman to William T. Sherman, October 1, 1862, CSHR 2/100, UNDA; Letter, Ellen Sherman to William T. Sherman, April 28, 1863, CSHR 2/105, UNDA; Letter, Ellen Sherman to William T. Sherman, March 7, 1863, CSHR 2/104, UNDA.

83. Letter (typescript), William T. Sherman Jr. to Ellen Sherman, January 2, 1863, CSHR 9/03, UNDA; Letter (typescript), William T. Sherman Jr. to William T. Sherman, May 1863, CSHR 9/03, UNDA.

84. Letter, Ellen Sherman to William T. Sherman, July 1, 1863, CSHR 2/108, UNDA.

85. Letter (typescript), William T. Sherman Jr. to William T. Sherman, May 1863, CSHR 9/03, UNDA; Brooks D. Simpson and Jean V. Berlin, eds., *Sherman's Civil War: Selected Correspondence of William T. Sherman, 1860–1865* (Chapel Hill: University of North Carolina Press, 1999), 316; Simpson and Berlin, *Sherman's Civil War*, 316, 263, 662.

86. Simpson and Berlin, *Sherman's Civil War*, 205, 422.

87. Letter, William T. Sherman to William T. Sherman Jr., June 21, 1863, CSHR 2/170, UNDA.

88. Letter, Ellen Sherman to William T. Sherman, June 8, 1863, CSHR 2/107, UNDA.

89. Letter, William T. Sherman to William T. Sherman Jr., June 21, 1863, CSHR 2/170, UNDA; Conyngham, "Soldiers of the Cross."

90. Conyngham, "Soldiers of the Cross."

91. Ibid.

92. Letter, William T. Sherman to William T. Sherman Jr., June 21, 1863, CSHR 2/170, UNDA; Simpson and Berlin, *Sherman's Civil War*, 521; Letter, Ellen Sherman to William T. Sherman, July 26, 1863, CSHR 2/108, UNDA.

93. Anna McAllister, *Ellen Ewing: Wife of General Sherman* (New York: Benziger Brothers, 1936), 264.

94. William T. Sherman, *Memoirs of General William T. Sherman*, vol. 1 (New York: D. Appleton & Co., 1886), 377, 373.

95. Letter, Ellen Sherman to William T. Sherman, October 1863 (n.d.), CSHR 2/109, UNDA.

96. McAllister, *Ellen Ewing*, 268.

97. Sherman, *Memoirs of General William T. Sherman*, 376.

98. Ellen Sherman to William T. Sherman, July 20, 1864, CSHR 2/114, UNDA; Letter, Ellen Sherman to William T. Sherman, August 16, 1864, CSHR 2/115, UNDA; Letter, Ellen Sherman to William T. Sherman, March 3, 1865, CSHR 2/120, UNDA; Letter, Ellen Sherman to William T. Sherman, March 7, 1865, CSHR 2/120, UNDA.

99. Hope, *Notre Dame*, 122.

CHAPTER 6

100. Corby, *Memoirs of Chaplain Life*, 159.

101. St. Clair A. Mulholland, *The Story of the 116th Regiment, Pennsylvania Infantry* (Philadelphia, PA: F.M. McManus, Jr,. & Co., 1899), 371–72. Mulholland's is the standard account of the scene, although he has been (gently) criticized—due to his talents as a storyteller—for "embroidering" the original over time. Still, Father Corby used Mulholland's account in his *Memoirs of Chaplain Life* but left out the admonition that the church refused Christian burial for deserters. Even if true, it seems uncharacteristic for the pastoral nature of the good chaplain. Father Corby related a separate but similar account of the absolution in a letter to Colonel John B. Bachelder, January 4, 1879, held by the Gettysburg National Military Park.

102. Mulholland, *Story of the 116th Regiment*, 372; Corby, *Memoirs of Chaplain Life*, 184.

103. Corby, *Memoirs of Chaplain Life*, 184; John F. Marszalek, "Call to Arms," *Notre Dame Magazine* 21, no. 3 (Fall 1992): 19; Corby, *Memoirs of Chaplain Life*, 185.

104. Corby, *Memoirs of Chaplain Life*, 186.

105. Ibid., xxi.

106. Ibid.

107. Letter, War Department to St. Clair A. Mulholland, August 12, 1893, IPAC.

108. Ibid.; Letter, St. Clair A. Mulholland to Father Corby, August 20, 1893, IPAC; Letter, James Quinlan to Father Corby, September 4, 1893, IPAC.

109. Corby, *Memoirs of Chaplain Life*, xxi; "A War Incident," poem by James J. Creswell, *Notre Dame Scholastic*, January 20, 1894, 279.

110. *Silver Jubilee of the University of Notre Dame* (Chicago, IL: E.B. Meyers, 1869), 164.

111. Letter, Orville Chamberlain to "Friends," August 19, 1862, Chamberlain Papers, Box 1, Folder 8, IHS.

112. Letter, Orville Chamberlain to General E.A. Carman, undated (postwar), Files, Chickamauga and Chattanooga National Military Park, Fort Oglethorpe, Georgia (hereafter CCNMP).

113. Ibid.

114. Letter, Orville Chamberlain to General E.A. Carman; Letter, Orville Chamberlain to General H.V. Boynton, November 26, 1895, Files, CCNMP.

115. Civil War Medal of Honor Citations, http://www.army.mil/medalofhonor/rubin/medal/citations1.htm; Eunice M. Barber, *The Wright-Chamberlin Genealogy: From Emigrant Ancestors to Present Generations* (Binghamton, NY: Vail-Ballou Company, 1914), 62.

116. Letter, Orville Chamberlain to father, October 16, 1863, Chamberlain Papers, Box 1, Folder 11, IHS.

CHAPTER 7

117. For an excellent discussion of the challenges faced by colleges and universities during the Civil War, and administration solutions to the challenges, see Willis Rudy, *The Campus and a Nation in Crisis: From the American Revolution to Vietnam* (Madison, NJ: Farleigh Dickinson University Press, 1996), 69–84.

118. Sorin, *Chronicles of Notre Dame du Lac*, 277–78.

119. Ibid., 277; James M. McCormack, typewritten essay of Notre Dame life during the Civil War and after, 1863–67, Notre Dame Student Collection (hereafter CNDS), 7/15, UNDA.

120. The author compiled statistics by year, state or foreign country using the UNDA "Index of Early Notre Dame Students, 1849–1912" at http://archives.nd.edu/search/students.htm. Admittedly, this was not a "scientific" survey, and some compromises were made. For example, each student was counted for each year they were enrolled; for some students this was a single year (they counted once), and for others it could be as many as five terms (they were counted five times). Furthermore, by including the orphan/destitute manual labor students—most of whom were from the Midwest—the percentage of "paying" students from the Confederate and Border States is likely underestimated.

121. McCormack, typewritten essay.

122. Sorin, *Chronicles of Notre Dame du Lac*, 285–86.

123. McCormack, typewritten essay.

124. Letter, Orville Chamberlain to Joseph Chamberlain, August 23, 1862, Chamberlain Papers, Box 1, Folder 8, IHS.

125. McCormack, typewritten essay.

126. Letter, Orville Chamberlain to "Friends," March 4, 1861, Chamberlain Papers, Box 1, Folder 8, IHS.
127. McCormack, typewritten essay; Hope, *Notre Dame*, 103.
128. Sorin, *Chronicles of Notre Dame du Lac*, 290–91.
129. Hope, *Notre Dame*, 118–19.
130. M. Georgia Costin, *Priceless Spirit: A History of the Sisters of the Holy Cross, 1841–1893* (Notre Dame, IN: University of Notre Dame Press, 1994), 192.
131. Ibid.
132. Ibid., 193.
133. Ibid.
134. *St. Joseph Valley Register* (Indiana), December 7, 1866, 3.
135. Ibid., December 13, 1866, 2.

CHAPTER 8

136. Sorin, *Chronicles of Notre Dame du Lac*, 288–89; Letter, Orville Chamberlain to "Father," September 12, 1864, Chamberlain Papers, Box 2, Folder 2, IHS.
137. Letter, Abraham Lincoln to William T. Sherman, September 19, 1864, Abraham Lincoln Papers, Library of Congress.
138. Rachael Sherman Thorndike, ed., *The Sherman Papers: Correspondence Between General and Senator Sherman from 1837 to 1891* (New York: Charles Scribner's Sons, 1894), 238; O'Connell, *Edward Sorin*, 453.
139. O'Connell, *Edward Sorin*, 496.
140. *OR*, ser. 3, vol. 3, 844–45.
141. Ibid., 845.
142. Thomas Low Nichols, *Forty Years of American Life* (London: Longman, Green, & Co., 1874), 299.
143. Willard H. Smith, *Schuyler Colfax: The Changing Fortunes of a Political Idol* (Indianapolis: Indiana Historical Bureau, 1952), 59; O'Connell, *Edward Sorin*, 501.
144. O'Connell, *Edward Sorin*, 500.
145. Smith, *Schuyler Colfax*, 198, 200.
146. O'Connell, *Edward Sorin*, 501.
147. Sorin, *Chronicles of Notre Dame du Lac*, 288–89; Dorothy O. Pratt, "Notre Dame and the Civil War Draft," unpublished manuscript, 15.

148. Sorin, *Chronicles of Notre Dame du Lac*, 289.

149. Ibid., 289.

150. Pratt, "Notre Dame and the Civil War Draft."

151. O'Connell, *Edward Sorin*, 503.

CHAPTER 9

152. Letter, Orville Chamberlain to Joseph Chamberlain, 1864, Chamberlain Papers, Box 2, Folder 2, IHS.

153. Corby, *Memoirs of Chaplain Life*, 216.

154. Ibid., 127.

155. Ibid., 236.

156. Sorin, *Chronicles of Notre Dame du Lac*, 292; Corby, *Memoirs of Chaplain Life*, 270–71.

157. *OR*, ser. 2, vol. 5, 382.

158. Ibid., ser. 1, vol. 34, pt. I, 339.

159. *Notre Dame Scholastic*, November 18, 1899, 181.

160. *OR*, ser. 1, vol. 45, pt. II, 158.

161. McAvoy, "War Letters of Father Peter Paul Cooney," 223–25.

162. Ibid., 224, 227.

163. Ibid., 227, 230, 229, 230.

164. Ibid., 230; *OR*, ser. 1, vol. 45, pt. I, 183, 198.

165. Petition, Officers/Soldiers of the 35th Indiana Infantry to Father Edward Sorin, January 30, 1865, Peter Paul Cooney Papers (CCOO), 1/07, UNDA.

166. Sorin, *Chronicles of Notre Dame du Lac*, 292.

167. "Letter, Orville Chamberlain to "Friends," July 7, 1864, Chamberlain Papers, Box 2, Folder 1, IHS; Letter, Orville Chamberlain to Joseph Chamberlain, September 12, 1864, Chamberlain Papers, Box 2, Folder 1, IHS.

168. Letter, Orville Chamberlain to Joseph Chamberlain, December 14, 1864, Chamberlain Papers, Box 2, Folder 2, IHS; Letter, Orville Chamberlain to Joseph Chamberlain, December 17, 1864, Chamberlain Papers, Box 2, Folder 2, IHS.

169. Letter, Orville Chamberlain to Joseph Chamberlain, April 20, 1865, Chamberlain Papers, Box 2, Folder 3, IHS.

170. Ibid.

171. Ibid.

CHAPTER 10

172. Clipping, *Chicago Evening Journal*, June 16, 1865, in "General Sherman at Notre Dame, Reception, Speeches," Notre Dame Printed and Reference Material Dropfiles (PDNP), Folder 1865/03, UNDA.

173. Ibid.

174. Ibid.

175. "General Sherman at Notre Dame"; Wilson D. Miscamble, ed., *Go Forth and Do Good: Memorable Notre Dame Commencement Addresses* (Notre Dame, IN: University of Notre Dame Press, 2003), 46–47.

176. *Notre Dame Scholastic*, March 31, 1906, 403.

177. Clipping, *St. Louis Post Dispatch*, October 6, 1897, Grand Army of the Republic Notre Dame Post 569 Records (CGAR), UNDA.

178. Letter, Brother John Chrysostom to Father Edward Sorin, June 5, 1887, IPAC.

179. Clipping, *St. Louis Star*, November 7, 1897, CGAR, UNDA.

180. *Notre Dame Scholastic*, October 9, 1897, 80–85.

181. Ibid.

182. Ibid.

183. *A Story of Fifty Years*, 112–13.

184. Minutes, December 29, 1897, CGAR, UNDA; resolution, CGAR, UNDA.

185. *Notre Dame Scholastic*, January 15, 1898, 264.

CONCLUSION

186. *Notre Dame Scholastic*, "Brother Raphael, G.A.R.," May 28, 1921, 488–89.

187. *OR*, ser. 1, vol. 23, 364–65; an excellent essay on the genesis of the guns, the misnomer of "Lady Davis" and their disposition can be found at John Ross, "Columbus, KY: Gibraltar of the West," http://rosswar.blogspot.com.

188. McAllister, *Flame in the Wilderness*, 201.

189. Eleanor C. Donnelly, *Crowned With Stars* (Notre Dame, IN: Notre Dame University, 1881), 129–31.

190. McAllister, *Flame in the Wilderness*, 341.

191. An excellent account of the development of the "Nuns of the Battlefield" monument can be found in Kathryn A. Jacob and Edwin

H. Remsberg (photographer), *Testament to Union: Civil War Monuments in Washington D.C.* (Baltimore, MD: Johns Hopkins University Press, 1998), 125–27.

192. Anthony Deahl, ed., *A Twentieth Century History and Biographical Record of Elkhart County, Indiana* (Chicago, IL: Lewis Publishing Company, 1906), 172.

193. Ibid., 173.

194. *Elkhart (IN) Review*, August 23, 1889, 2–3.

195. Ibid.

196. Ibid.

197. Ibid.; "A Monumental Rededication," *Elkhart (IN) Truth*, A1, A9, n.d.

198. *Gettysburg (PA) Compiler*, November 2, 1910, 1; Letter, St. Clair Mulholland to Brother Leander, December 23, 1907, CGAR, UNDA.

199. *Father Corby at Gettysburg* (Philadelphia, PA: McManus, circa 1909), 7.

200. *Gettysburg (PA) Compiler*, November 2, 1910, 1.

201. Ibid.

202. *Adams County News* (Gettysburg, Pennsylvania), November 5, 1910, 1.

203. *Notre Dame Scholastic*, June 3, 1911, 548; Corby, *Memoirs of Chaplain Life*, 400.

204. *Notre Dame Scholastic*, June 3, 1911, 548.

ABOUT THE AUTHOR

A chemist by education and profession, Jim Schmidt is currently employed as a pharmaceutical research scientist near Houston, Texas. Jim has had a lifelong interest in history and has written more than fifty articles for the *Civil War News* and *North & South*, *World War II*, *Learning Through History* and *Chemical Heritage* magazines. He is the author of two previous books on the American Civil War and has given presentations on history to groups across the Midwest and mid-Atlantic. Jim Schmidt is an active member of the Woodlands (TX) Civil War Round Table and the National Museum of Civil War Medicine.

Visit us at
www.historypress.net